DATE DUE

			PRINTED IN U.S.A.
GAYLORD			

William Jefferson Clinton

42nd President of
the United States

"As far as the Presidency is concerned," states Clinton, *"I'd like to be remembered as a leader who left Americans happier, healthier, and safer than they were before I came to this office."* (Associated Press.)

William Jefferson Clinton

42nd President of the United States

David R. Collins

IHM18355
17.26

 GARRETT EDUCATIONAL CORPORATION

Cover: *Official presidential photographic portrait of William Jefferson Clinton.*
(The White House)

Manufactured in the United States of America

Library of Congress Cataloging-in-Publication Data

Collins, David R.
  William Jefferson Clinton: 42nd president of the United States /
by David R. Collins.
    p. cm. - (Presidents of the United States)
  Includes bibliographical references (p.   ) and index.
  ISBN 1-56074-056-6 (libr. edn.)
    1. Clinton, Bill, 1946-   – Juvenile literature. 2. Presidents–
United States – Biography – Juvenile literature. [1. Clinton, Bill,
1946-   . 2. Presidents.] I. Title. II. Series.
E886.C655   1995
973.929'092–dc20
[B]   95-852
                                                        CIP
                                                         AC

Contents

Chronology for
William Jefferson Clinton

1946   Born August 19 in Hope, Arkansas

1964   Graduated from Hot Springs High School

1968   Graduated from Georgetown University, Washington, D.C.; named Rhodes scholar, attended Oxford University

1973   Graduated from Yale University of Law, New Haven, Connecticut

1974   Ran for U.S. House of Representatives, was defeated

1975   Married Hillary Rodham on October 11

1975-1976   Taught law at the University of Arkansas

1976   Elected Attorney General of Arkansas

1978   Elected Governor of Arkansas

1980   Daughter Chelsea born February 27; defeated in re-election bid for governorship of Arkansas

1980-1982   Worked for law firm of Wright, Lindsey and Jennings

1982   Re-elected Governor of Arkansas

1983-1992   Served as Governor of Arkansas

1992   Elected President of the United States on November 3

1993   Inaugurated January 20, 1993 as the forty-second President of the United States

Chapter 1

A Sad Ending, A "Hopeful" Beginning

"We have just received word that President John F. Kennedy has been shot in Dallas, Texas. Reports are that shots were fired at a motorcade in downtown Dallas and that the president was hit. We will present more details as soon as they become available." With those words, the world learned of an American tragedy–the assassination of the president.

On a November afternoon in 1963, Americans across the country sat glued to their television sets and radios, listening for more news about the shooting in Dallas. For many, the thought of the vibrant and energetic Kennedy failing victim to an assassin's bullet was too unbelievable to accept.

ACCEPTING THE SHOCK

The news of the Dallas shooting was especially shocking to one high school senior in Hot Springs, Arkansas. Seventeen-year-old Bill Clinton could not believe the news.

"Of course, millions of people respected and loved President Kennedy," Clinton reflected years later. "But on November 22, 1963, many of us who were in high school felt we had lost much more than a national leader. Kennedy's youth was always emphasized, and although he was older in our eyes, we identified with his youthfulness and his sense of direction. He believed in serving and reaching out. He wanted

1

people to help themselves, not just look for help from others."

Only four months before the shooting in Dallas, Bill Clinton had had the chance to meet President Kennedy. It was a meeting that sparked a dedicated interest in politics within the boy from Hot Springs.

Not that there weren't clues about that interest along the way. From the moment he entered the world, the future president seemed to be a "people person." Yet unlike his predecessor and idol John F. Kennedy, the boy from Hope, Arkansas, did not enjoy the privileges that wealth and family position provide.

Turmoil and Tragedy

Bill's parents were married in Shreveport, Louisiana, in 1941, shortly before the United States was pulled into World War II. Virginia Cassidy was a nurse and William Jefferson Blythe III sold cars. In 1942, Blythe joined the war effort. When he returned to the United States after the war ended in 1945, the ex-serviceman had trouble landing a job. The best he could do was selling heavy equipment in Chicago. When Virginia became pregnant, she moved in with her parents in the small town of Hope, Arkansas. Blythe made plans to bring her north to be with him.

On a stormy night in May, 1946, Blythe made the familiar trip south to Hope. Finally, he was ready to bring his wife to Chicago when he returned. But it was not to be. Without warning, a tire blew out near Sikeston, Missouri, sending the car into a ditch. Hurled from the car, Blythe was killed instantly.

Virginia Blythe, six months pregnant, was grief-stricken. Yet she resolved to be "doubly strong" since her baby would only have one parent. The baby arrived August 19, 1946. His mother named him William Jefferson Blythe IV after the father he had never known and would never meet.

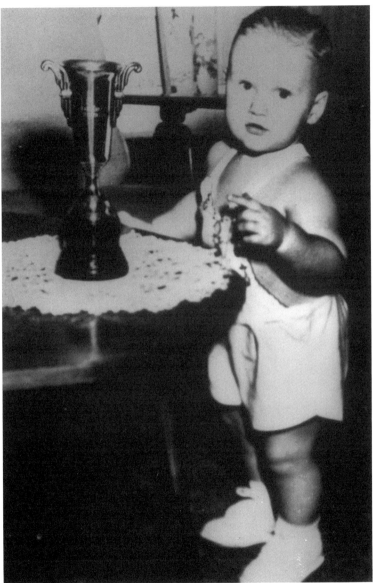

Pictured here at eighteen months, young Billy Blythe stayed with his grandparents in Arkansas while his widowed mother, Virginia, headed to New Orleans, Louisiana for training as a nurse-anesthetist. (Associated Press.)

Surrounded by Love

Billy was a happy baby, enjoying the constant attention of a loving mother and doting grandparents. But by the time the boy was two, Virginia knew she needed to go back to school, to update her nursing skills and get a better paying job. She headed back to Louisiana where she began studying to become a nurse-anestheist. Baby Billy was left at home with her parents.

Eldridge and Edith Cassidy were simple, hardworking people who ran a small grocery story and tried to save their money. Neither of them had gone to college, but they recognized the importance of a good education.

They read to their grandson, and as soon as he knew letters and words, he read to them. They played number games, teaching him to add and subtract. They might not have an indoor toilet, yet they did have a desire to raise a bright and well-loved grandson. From his grandfather, Billy Blythe learned a lot about how to treat people. Many of the customers who came to the Cassidy grocery store had little money. "You can pay me as soon as you get the money," Eldridge Cassidy would say. "I'll put the amount down now and cross it off later." Folks in the neighborhood appreciated the man's kindness, and the small boy at his grandfather's side learned from it, too.

OFF TO SCHOOL

Four-year-old Billy Blythe was eager to start kindergarten. Mary and Nannie Perkins, two sisters dedicated to the teaching profession, operated their school in a small white clapboard house in their backyard. Each day a T-shirted, blue-jeaned, and cowboy-booted Billy Blythe displayed his beginning skills at reading and arithmetic and knowing everyone's name.

One lunchtime proved especially eventful for the lively Billy Blythe. A group of boys decided to try a little high jumping, stretching a rope and seeing who could leap over it. Each time the boys hoisted the rope a bit, Billy jumped. He cleared the rope again and again, but finally his cowboy heel caught. Down he went! The pain was agonizing, as Billy cried and wailed. The Perkins sisters called for Billy's grandparents, who came and took the boy to the hospital. Sadly, the leg was broken in three places, an injury requiring a plastic cast up to his hip with full suspension in the air.

Another Father Enters the Scene

Life changed greatly for Billy Blythe in 1950. His mother, back from her nursing studies in New Orleans, met and began dating Roger Clinton, the local Buick salesman. In 1950, the two were married. Three years later, when Billy was seven, the family moved to Hot Springs, where Roger's brother owned a car dealership.

Like many families in the area, the Clintons were devout Southern Baptists. But Virginia knew the fine reputation of the local Catholic grade school. She reasoned that it would be easier for Billy, who had attended the tiny schools of Hope, to move into the much bigger Hot Springs Schools if he first went to St. John's Catholic Elementary. Billy brought home fine grades until one day when he displayed a "D" in conduct. Virginia Clinton paid the school a visit. "He's just so competitive," Billy's teachers told the concerned mother. "He answers questions before he gets called upon. He must learn to wait his turn. Maybe a "D" will make him think twice."

The "D" plan worked. The thought that he might make enemies by being so aggressive made Billy display better conduct. He started waiting for other students to answer. He gave his own answers more thought. Soon he had raised that "D" to an "A."

"Hot Dog!"

In the fourth grade, Billy joined the public school system. At Ramble Elementary, He made friends quickly. He coined a favorite expression, "Hot Dog!" and used it whenever he got excited. The phrase caught on like wildfire, and soon students throughout the school were using it.

Always prepared for his classwork, Billy loved on competition. He was too chunky to run fast, but he still tried hard to win at football and baseball. He took the same energy and spirit into a game of Monopoly or cards.

During recess at school, Billy earned a reputation as peacemaker. "Here comes Billy!" someone would yell, and often playground fights would simply dissolve. It wasn't that he was so tough physically, but rather that everybody wanted to be his friend and keep him happy. Fights did not make Billy Blythe happy.

Trouble at Home

But at home the fights were not so easy to stop. Roger Clinton was an alcoholic. When he was sober, he worked hard at selling cars and was a loving, caring person. But when he began drinking, he became angry and even violent. He took much of his frustration out on his wife. More than once Virginia wore bruises from her husband's alcoholic outbursts. Once he became so out of control he fired a gun in the living room. The police hauled him off to jail.

It was no surprise that young Billy Blythe enjoyed breaking up fights on the school grounds. "It wasn't just the littler kids Billy would stop from fighting," one teacher remembered. "He wasn't afraid to step in when some of the older and bigger boys got into a scuffle."

By the time he was fourteen, Billy Blythe had had enough of his stepfather's abusive behavior at home. Hearing Roger

Clinton yelling and slapping his wife around, a sturdy and rugged Billy broke down their bedroom door. The determined teenager motioned to his mother and stepbrother behind him and glared at his stepfather. "You will never hit either one of them again," the boy warned. "If you want them, you'll have to go through me." There was no mistaking the force and sincerity of that warning. From that day on, Roger Clinton, Sr. stopped physically abusing his family.

However, his drinking did not stop. Virginia sought a divorce from Roger Clinton and won. Yet, only three months later, he managed to convince her to take him back and they remarried. In 1960, as "an expression of family solidarity," Billy legally changed his name from William Blythe to William Clinton.

SCHOOL DAYS, SCHOOL DAZE

Although he had many friends in entering Hot Springs High School, Bill Clinton kept his family problems to himself. Instead, his teachers and peers knew him as a super saxophone player, a dedicated Boy Scout, and a skillful classroom debater. He brought school discussions home, where he and his mother sat around the kitchen table thrashing out ideas and opinions about issues of the day. When her duties as a nurse and anestheist pulled her away from home, she hired housekeepers to look after her two sons.

"Virginia took her role as mother very seriously," a family friend noted. "She worked because it would help the family, not because she wanted luxuries for herself. Even when the family bought a television set, it was largely because Virginia thought it would help the boys learn."

The television set did exactly that. Bill Clinton was fascinated by special news broadcasts and interviews with famous people. The political conventions were hypnotic. He wanted to hear every word.

A Hero Appears

No one on television captivated the impressionable young Clinton more than President John F. Kennedy. Whenever the chief executive was addressing Congress or the nation, Bill Clinton was watching and listening. The boy studied the leader's every gesture, soaked in every word he said, and chuckled at Kennedy's quick wit.

In 1963, Clinton got a chance to meet his idol face to face. Selected to attend Boys State, a state camp set up to bring high school boys and girls together to study grass-roots politics, Bill ran as a delegate to Boys Nation. Those elected traveled to Washington where they met national elected officials and visited the White House.

Young Clinton won the election. In a July jaunt to the nation's capitol, the sixteen-year-old boy from Hot Springs visited all the historic sites. He lunched with Senator J. William Fullbright, a Democrat from Arkansas, in the Senate dining room. Fullbright was the chairman of the powerful Senate Foreign Relations Department.

But the biggest thrill for Bill Clinton was getting to meet President Kennedy. As the chief executive mingled with guests in the White House Rose Garden, Clinton went up and extended his hand. Kennedy smiled and nodded, exchanging warm greetings.

FINDING A DIRECTION

Once he returned to Hot Springs, Bill Clinton knew what direction his life would take. He set aside past thoughts of becoming a Baptist minister, a teacher, or a professional musician. A new ambition had taken hold of him. "When he came back from Washington," his mother recalled, "holding this picture of himself with Jack Kennedy, and the expression on his face, I knew right then that politics was the answer for

While visiting the White House as part of a Boys Nation delegation in the summer of 1963, Bill Clinton got the chance to meet President John F. Kennedy. After that meeting, Clinton's mother declared that her son knew politics was the answer for him. (Associated Press.)

him."

With memories of meeting President Kennedy four months before still etched in his mind, Bill Clinton learned of the shooting of his hero. Soon afterward, the Hot Springs senior learned that the President of the United States was dead. "In a strange way, I took the loss of President Kennedy very personally," Bill Clinton recalled years later. "He helped to shape my hopes and dreams. One suffers a lot when an individual like that is suddenly and tragically gone from your life." While a nation sadly mourned the death of a fallen president, a new spirit was born within a young man in Arkansas. For the first time in his life, Bill Clinton felt determined to make Kennedy's words live, to ask not what his country could do for him, but what he could do for his country.

Chapter 2

Charting a Course

As Bill Clinton strolled across the stage to receive his high school diploma in 1964, he could point to a variety of achievements. Academically, he ranked fourth in a class of 323 students, having won recognition as a National Merit semifinalist. Musically, he was an instrumental standout, having displayed his saxophone talents in the concert band, the marching band, the pep band, and stage band. He had won honors in the All-State First Band. Theatrically, he had won accolades and applause as a lead in dramatic productions such as *Arsenic and Old Lace* and served as an emcee in talent shows. In the leadership arena, he'd served as his class president, Beta Club president, and Junior Classical League president. As far as colleges were concerned, his high school record would open many doors.

HEADING EAST

Clinton knew exactly which door he wanted to open. Georgetown University's School of Foreign Service in Washington, D. C. offered a curriculum tailor-made for his wishes. Not only were courses offered in international and international relations on campus, the school offered students chances to travel and take subjects all over the world. The possibilities delighted Clinton.

In the fall of 1964, a young man with a fresh crewcut

Already climbing the political ladder, Bill Clinton was elected sophomore class president at Georgetown University. He poses here for a 1966 yearbook picture with secretary Andy Poole in the middle and vice-president Terry Modlin on the right. Modlin beat Clinton in the race for the senior class presidency, but classmates were already predicting Clinton would someday be the nation's president. (Associated Press.)

arrived on the campus of Georgetown University. Bill Clinton was eager to start on his studies, yet he knew he would need some extra income to cover his expenses. A call to the office of Senator Fullbright from Arkansas found him speaking to a top assistant. Clinton laid out his situation, hoping there might be some work available.

"We don't have a full-time job," explained Lee Williams, "but we do have two part-time slots."

Clinton listened attentively as Williams explained the duties of the positions. His attention increased when Fullbright's aide mentioned the salaries involved. One of the jobs paid $5000 a year, while the other paid $3500.

"I'll take them both," Clinton answered with confidence.

"You're just the guy I'm looking for," Williams replied.

Getting Down to Business

Clinton threw himself into a busy schedule at Georgetown. Most of the other students were from fancy prep schools and big cities. But Bill Clinton openly admitted he was a small town boy with bigtime hopes. He impressed his teachers with his quick mind and penetrating questions, while charming his peers with his sense of humor and leadership. His classmates elected Clinton as their class president.

Working for Senator Fullbright gave Bill Clinton an opportunity to know what troubled the folks back in Arkansas. He helped sort the mail as it came in. People shared their thoughts about the fighting going on in Vietnam, urging President Lyndon Johnson to bring an end to the war. They wrote about the struggle between blacks and whites, a battle that was still being waged even after the passage of the Civil Rights Bill in 1964. Bill Clinton already had strong feelings about that topic. While many Arkansas residents felt blacks deserved the same rights as whites, they wanted the two races kept separate, especially in schools. Not Clinton. "All Americans should have the same rights," he argued, "and that includes learning and living side by side regardless of race." The people wrote about unemployment, welfare, and women's rights. Reading the letters and seeking information to help the people gave Clinton a better understanding of the people of his native state.

Forgetting the Past

Over the years Clinton had also gained a real understanding of his stepfather's disease, alcoholism. When that ailment was compounded by cancer and Roger Clinton came east for treatment, Bill Clinton traveled every weekend to Duke University in North Carolina. It was a 250 mile drive, but Bill Clinton did not mind. The days of fighting were over. Before his stepfather died, the two men mended their strained relationship from the past.

At Georgetown, Clinton plunged deeply into his classwork. In his economics classes, he not only analyzed facts and statistics, he offered solutions for improving existing financial conditions. Shrewd diplomacy, Clinton determined, was the secret to maintaining relations among nations of the world. He learned to recognize the importance of a strong family unit to create national strength and unity. "Bill Clinton was never content to merely scrape the surface of ideas and issues," one of his professors noted. "He wanted to get to the core of problems, to understand the nature of government and people."

Reaching Out

In 1968, Clinton got a firsthand view of how frustrated some people could become. Following the assassination of Martin Luther King Jr., race riots broke out in many major American cities. Clinton and another friend from Hot Springs, Carolyn Staley, volunteered to drive Red Cross ambulances through strifetorn neighborhoods of Washington, D.C. They wore hats and scarves to hide the color of their skin. The sight of people looting stores and burning buildings and vehicles etched a permanent place in Bill Clinton's mind.

"About this time I think Bill also became convinced that the quality of education played a big role in how people behaved," Staley noted. "He felt sure that Arkansas needed better trained teachers and better programs for reaching the young. He promised that if he ever had the chance, he would work toward that goal."

Clinton's high grades paid off. By the time he was a senior, his academic achievements had earned him the right to apply for a Rhodes scholarship. It was a chance to go to England and take classes at the prestigious Oxford University. "I hated the thought of Bill being so far away," Virginia Clinton remembered. "And yet, I knew how badly he wanted to go. So naturally, I hoped and prayed that he would be picked."

AHOY, ENGLAND!

Bill <u>was</u> picked. In the fall of 1968, he sailed for England with thirty-two other Rhodes scholars. He decided to pursue a graduate degree in politics.

The change in geography afforded a major change in culture too. Bill soon discovered that the British were much more reserved, even standoffish. By now, the young man from Arkansas was an imposing physical presence, weighing 230 pounds and standing 6'2". He'd let his hair grow longer, in keeping with the influence of the Beatles, the four singing British superstars, and his walk reflected a confident swagger and poise. His broad smile came quickly, followed by a hearty handshake and an "I'm Bill Clinton" that registered immediate friendliness. Although he was a long way from home, he certainly showed few signs of homesickness. In truth, Bill Clinton appeared right at home wherever he went, and he was more than willing to share stories of the United States in general, and Arkansas in particular. "You ought to see our apple blossoms," he'd declare. "They're fluffier and whiter than any clouds you ever saw. And they have the sweetest scent you've ever smelled." Yes, there was no modesty when Bill Clinton talked about Hope and Hot Springs.

Discussing World Problems

Not only were the classes challenging at Oxford, but Clinton discovered the late-night talk sessions offered a chance for the exchange of many ideas. Vietnam was a frequent topic. Oxford students from Britain were full of questions, and they often sought out the gregarious young Clinton. Protesters back in the United States demanded the end of American involvement in the Vietnam War. Clinton studied the situation and discussed it with others. He became more and more convinced that his country did not belong in Vietnam and should get out. He spoke out loud and often against United States involvement. When he traveled away from the Oxford campus into other countries–there were many courses which allowed students a chance to pick up credits through travel– Clinton was asked about Vietnam. Again he shared his firm belief that America should get out of Vietnam immediately. He even helped to organize antiwar rallies.

Dealing With the Draft

Ironically, about this time Clinton received a notice from his draft board to report for induction into the service. But the date to report had already passed. Clinton sought advice from the board and they granted him a student deferment. It was only a temporary solution, however, and Clinton did not want military service to interrupt his education. He signed up with the Army Reserve Officer Training Corps (ROTC) back home in Fayetteville, Arkansas. That way, he could fulfill his military obligations through classes and training while attending the University of Arkansas Law School.

Yet Clinton soon changed his mind and cancelled the ROTC agreement. He threw himself back into the draft lottery and returned to Oxford to continue his studies. The Selective Service System, after numerous attempts to find a fair lottery method, decided to use birthdates as the way to determine the order for drafting eligible candidates. On December 1, 1969, the numbers were drawn. Clinton's number was 311. He knew he was not likely to be drafted.

REACHING INTO NEW WORLDS

Clinton thrived in the academic arena of Oxford. If he wasn't reading a book, he was debating ideas. He not only attended the classes in which he was enrolled but sat in on other lectures and presentations. "His mind would never shut down," remembered one of his classmates. "He loved to talk about the ideal society, a utopia where people lived and worked with vitality and purpose." Another student recalled Clinton's eager, competitive spirit: "At Georgetown, Bill was wrapped up with curricular and extracurricular activities. At Oxford, he just wanted to soak up as much learning as he could. He read constantly, about three hundred books a year, and he was always wanting to discuss new ideas." During this time the ever-curious Clinton also experimented with marijuana, an experimentation that would come back to haunt him years later.

As he approached the end of his second year at Oxford, Bill Clinton faced a big decision. He could have another year studying in England under the terms of his Rhodes Scholarship or he could accept a scholarship to Yale Law School. The young man from Arkansas weighed the choice with great care.

Then he made his decision.

Chapter 3

Her Name was Hillary

In the fall of 1971, Bill Clinton enrolled as a student at the Yale Law School in New Haven, Connecticut. He was hardly the traditional law student at the institution. Most of his classmates came from wealthy families, many boasting direct ties to oldtime colonial bluebloods. Many within the Yale student body had attended private Eastern prep schools and were expected to take over prestigious law practices someday. Clinton's future was uncertain, but he knew what he had to do at Yale. "I would have to study hard to keep my scholarship and find a job to help pay the bills," he remembered. The studying part was challenging, yet the "longhaired young liberal" as Clinton labeled himself, threw himself into his classes with zest and zeal.

Financially, the 25-year-old man from Arkansas managed to get a loan to help out his scholarship. He shuffled a variety of jobs, most of them related to government. A city councilman in Hartford hired him to do minor political tasks, while a lawyer in New Haven assigned Clinton to help investigate civil law cases. There was a dangerous element in the latter work, especially when he had to visit rundown tenements. He saw people shooting up heroin and shooting at each other, people whose lives were out of control and desperately needed help. Such sights steered him toward a more active role in Connecticut politics. " I wanted to help, to be useful,"

Clinton recalled. "But first I had to learn and law and find out how I could reach people in need."

Starting at the Grass Roots

Clinton's first personal encounter with grass-roots political campaigning came when Democrat Joe Duffy made a run for the United States Senate. Juggling his classes with volunteer work, Clinton handed out campaign literature, answered phones, and went door to door in Duffy's behalf. The smile and handshake came readily to Clinton, and he knew his candidate's background and ideas inside and out. Duffy held town meetings, sharing his goals with four or four hundred people, whoever would turn out to listen. Clinton sat attentively, soaking in every word his candidate uttered, and noting how that message affected the crowd. Duffy lost the election, but he won in the district where Bill Clinton had worked. "It was like an appetizer," he said later, " and I longed for the time when I could speak for myself in a campaign."

In the meantime, there was much to learn. Corporate law, criminal law, international law–the note-taking, the lectures, the tests and exams–the more grueling the schedule, the more Clinton appeared to blossom. All-night studying sessions became the rule rather than the exception, and when Clinton wasn't in his campus room, he was in the law library.

Not that Clinton never socialized. He shared a beach house with two other students, and they entertained whenever they could afford to invite friends in. With a Carole King record on the stereo and chicken frying on the stove, Bill Clinton was a perfect host. Of course, guests often heard countless stories about the grand and glorious state of Arkansas, but most were willing to pay the price.

CHANCE MEETING?

One day, while Clinton was extolling the virtues of Hope

and Hot Springs for a small crowd in the Yale student lounge, another student named Hillary Rodham stopped to listen for a moment. "And not only that, we have the largest watermelons in the world!" Clinton declared. The woman asked her companions who the fellow was. "Oh, that's Bill Clinton, and all he ever talks about is Arkansas."

Hailing from the exclusive Chicago suburb of Park Ridge, Illinois, the bouncy and bright Rodham knew little about Arkansas. Maybe the folks there <u>did</u> grow the largest watermelons in the world. Whatever the case, the young blond graduate from Wellesley College was more than mildly intrigued by the long-haired handsome fellow from Arkansas. He might be worth knowing better.

Within a few days that opportunity presented itself at the Yale Law School Law Library. While talking to a friend, Bill Clinton kept noticing Hillary Rodham at a nearby desk that was stacked high with books and notepads. Although he tried to concentrate on what his buddy was saying, it was clear Clinton was distracted. In a while, the focus of his attention walked over. "Look," declared the confident Rodham, "if you're going to keep staring at me and I'm going to keep staring back, we should at least introduce ourselves."

From that initial encounter, Bill Clinton and Hillary Rodham became a partnership, whether it was sharing coffee and conversation in the lounge or exchanging lecture notes and ideas in study sessions. Clinton was dazzled by Hillary's quick mind and directness. Student body president at Wellesley, she had graduated from the prestigious women's college in 1969. Unlike some of her female counterparts, Hillary was not at Yale Law School to land a man with a promising future in law. She was a force to be reckoned with herself, and she constantly challenged Bill Clinton's intellect with her analytical thinking and forceful opinions.

Helping a Candidate

Clinton and Rodham headed for Texas in the summer of 1972. Democrat George McGovern was challenging Republican Richard Nixon for the presidency, and the two Yale students were eager to test their political savvy in the national campaign. While Hillary registered Hispanic voters in San Antonio, Bill helped take charge of McGovern's state headquarters in Austin.

Votes were not won by merely sitting at a desk, and no one knew that better than Bill Clinton. He relished sitting down and bantering with potential McGovern supporters at every opportunity. At campaign headquarters, Clinton kept the volunteer helpers hyped up. Whether it was playing a pickup game of touch football or munching on tacos, McGovern's young lieutenant at the Austin headquarters kept his political teammates energetic and willing to put in every extra hour possible. "I recognized then his very special qualities," observed an Austin co-worker Judy Trabuiski. "He reflected leadership, commitment, passion and compassion–and I knew he could make a difference in this country."

Despite the fact that Bill and Hillary had not attended any classes at Yale during the term, they hurried back to campus to take their final tests. They managed to score top grades.

But it was not only on exam papers that Bill Clinton and Hillary Rodham flexed their legal knowledge and know-how. When they teamed up for Yale's yearly trial competition, they proved a dynamic duo. While Clinton displayed his gentlemanly slow style and grace in mock courtroom situations, Rodham was direct and aggressive. One observer attributed their differences to regional backgrounds–Clinton being the ever well-mannered Southerner, Rodham representing the "cut to the heart of the matter" Midwesterner. Whatever the case, the couple showed flair and depth in their delivery of arguments and summations of ideas.

In 1972 Senator George McGovern carried the Democratic banner for U.S. President. A fulltime law student at Yale, Bill Clinton took some time off from his studies to help in the campaign, and here he meets and greets the candidate at the Little Rock Airport. (Associated Press.)

HEADING HOME

As Clinton completed his studies at Yale, job offers flowed in. Many were from prestigious law firms promising handsome financial rewards and rapid advancement. The Judiciary Committee of the U.S. House of Representatives was looking for legal help investigating President Richard Nixon and the complicated Watergate affair. Hillary Rodham jumped at the chance to join the investigation. But Bill Clinton had other plans. At twenty-six, he headed home to Arkansas. "All I wanted to do was go home," he declared. "I thought I would hang out my shingle in Hot Springs and see if I could run for public office."

Clinton had his work cut out for him. Economically, educationally, culturally–in just about every way possible, Arkansas was ranked at the bottom of the totem pole. In 1973, with the ink still wet on his law degree, Bill Clinton promised his mother he would "break his back" to help the state prosper, if the people would support him.

But at first, Bill Clinton knew he had to find a means to support himself. When he applied for a job teaching at the University of Arkansas Law School in Fayetteville, the dean labeled him too young. "I've been too young to do everything I've ever done," the undaunted Clinton quipped, then went for an interview and got the job.

Some people would have curled right up in Fayetteville and spent the rest of their lives teaching at the respected law school there. Nestled in the picturesque Ozark Mountains, the community enjoyed a peaceful flow of living, protected from the hectic pace of larger areas. Despite the satisfaction Clinton found in teaching, another force stirred within. The political bug bit him and would not let go.

Challenging the People

The Third Congressional District in Arkansas rested firmly in the hands of Republican John Paul Hammerschmidt. The chances of any Democrat snagging that position were slim indeed. Few were willing to try, yet Bill Clinton jumped into the battle. "I hadn't planned to get into politics so soon," Clinton admitted later. "But the Democrats needed a candidate, and I always enjoyed a challenge."

Many people were surprised at the well-thought-out campaign the newcomer waged. Clinton was glad to be able to work from his own ideas for a change, not merely speaking in behalf of someone else. He advocated a new national health insurance program, fairer taxes, public funding of national elections, and more power to the people. He won the Democratic primary election, thereby gaining the right to take on Hammerschmidt. The Democratic Party's finances were sparse for Clinton's campaign budget, and his own bankroll was even more slender. He traveled through the twenty-one counties of the district in his car, talking before any group who would listen. He organized many of the teachers at the Fayetteville Law School to work for him. "He shot us full of life and togetherness," noted one professor.

Hillary Rodham, fresh from working with the House Judiciary Committee in Washington, arrived to teach at the University of Arkansas Law School–and to lend her counsel and support to Clinton's campaign. The candidate met her plane in Little Rock. What was usually a one-hour trip to the Clinton family home in Hot Springs turned into a nine-hour tour of countless Arkansas attractions, with frequent stops for a piece or two of a friend's pie. It was clear that the blossoming young political candidate from Arkansas and the young woman from Illinois shared more than a love of politics.

Making a Pledge

As for Clinton's political message, he carried a message of fiscal responsibility to the public. "I pledge to watch every penny that is spent," he told the voters. "There can be no more reckless pork-barreling in Congress. Tax dollars will be directed to that which will truly help the country as a whole."

Labeled "a brilliant young law professor" by the Arkansas Gazette, the newspaper endorsed Clinton's new and dynamic ideas. He won the backing of the state's educational association, the group citing his "consistent stand of the issues affecting the quality of education in Arkansas" as well as his demand for more federal funds for reforms.

At the beginning of the campaign, pollsters predicted a landslide for Hammerschmidt. By the time election day ar-

Clinton's Three Favorite Ladies

"Behind every successful man there's a woman." That familiar maxim has been around far longer than the feminist movement seeking rights for women. Whether one accepts the idea or rejects it, President Bill Clinton attributes much of what he is as a person today to three women in his life - his mother, his wife, and his daughter.

In accepting the nomination for the presidency, Clinton addressed the Democratic delegates attending their party convention and millions of people watching on television. But largely, he spoke directly to his mother, Virginia Kelley, who sat in a special seating area reserved for dignitaries. The woman dabbed often at her tear-filled eyes. "My mother taught me," the Democratic nominee declared. "She taught me about family and hard work and sacrifice. She held steady through tragedy after tragedy."

The tough times began early for Virginia, whose first husband died in an automobile accident when she was pregnant with the baby who would eventually be elected to the top office in the nation. She married four more times, twice to the same abusive husband. A colorful personality, she loved the racetrack and shared quick and zany wisetracks with reporters. She died of cancer in January of 1994 at the age of 70. "She was a courageous fighter all her life," noted the President, "and whatever good qualities I have today, she helped to put there."

Throughout his public career, President Clinton has been singled out as an advocate for children and youth. He credits his wife, Hillary Rodham Clinton, with instilling a deep and sincere love for young people. "She taught me that all children can learn," he states, "and that each of us has a duty to help them do it."

The President and his wife met while they were attending Yale University Law School. Hailing from Park Ridge, Illinois, she had attended Wellesley College, where she served as student body president her senior year and graduated with high honors in 1969. Never known for her timidity, Hillary made the first move toward Clinton, after noticing the man from Arkansas watching her in the library. "Look," she declared, "if you're going to keep staring at me, and I'm going to keep staring back, I think we should at least know each other. I'm Hillary Rodham. What's your name?"

With that introduction, the two Yale students went on to share personal and political adventures which united in marriage on October 1 1, 1975. "Hillary has a brilliant mind and a warm, compassionate heart," says Clinton. "She is my greatest asset as a loving partner." Despite regular displays of affection in public, reports of heated exchanges between the President and the First Lady occasionally surface in the media. 'When you care about someone, you squabble now and then," explained the President's mother, Virginia Clinton Kelley. "There's often a lot of love in a good old-fashioned squabble."

Both Bill and Hillary Clinton have worked hard to keep their daughter Chelsea out of the public spotlight. "It's not her fault that she is in the situation she is in," the President states. "I want Chelsea to enjoy growing up and to have the best childhood we can offer." As to what he tries to provide his daughter, Clinton answers "unconditional love, self esteem and discipline."

Born February 27, 1980, while her father was in his second term as governor of Arkansas, Chelsea has always been near the center of political activity. Before Clinton assumed the presidency, the young girl was often photographed with the family pet cat "Socks." The Clintons' decision to send their daughter to private schools caused a minor flap with critics who asked, "What's wrong with public education?" But the controversy died quickly, most people accepting that it would be difficult to offer protection to the daughter of a President at a public school — and that despite Bill Clinton's position, this was a family matter. Although sheltered from the media, Chelsea received considerable attention —and more than a few accolades — when she appeared on a Washington, D. C. stage in the ballet "The Nutcracker."

"I never knew my own father," President Clinton recalls. "I want to make sure I spend as much time with my daughter as I can. She's very special to me, and she keeps me in tune with what the younger folks are thinking."

rived in November of 1974, the race was a dead heat. The incumbent barely squeaked by, with challenger Clinton capturing 48.2 per cent of the vote. Hammerschmidt returned to the House, but Bill Clinton had proved himself a force to be reckoned with. "We'll be hearing more from this young man," observed one newspaper editor.

Clinton was delighted with his strong showing. He had not expected to win, but he was grateful at the opportunity to "experiment" with politics by actually running in an election. He knew he would run again.

Another Kind of Race

Clinton also knew there was something else he wanted to win other than a political office. He wanted Hillary Rodham. They spent more and more time together, sharing their ideas and hopes and dreams.

One day, when Bill Clinton picked Hillary up at the airport, he had a surprise waiting. He didn't drive her back to her apartment in Fayetteville. Instead, he took her to prairie-style bungalow on California Drive.

"I've bought that house you like," Clinton said.

"What house I like?" asked Hillary.

"You know. Remember when we were driving around the day before you left and there was a For Sale sign and you said, 'Gee, that's a nice house?'"

"Bill, that's all I said. I've never been inside it."

"Well, I thought you liked it, so I bought it. So I guess we have to get married now."

It was an unusual proposal, certainly not out of any "how to" book. Yet it worked. Hillary said yes.

Taking the Big Step

After such a unique proposal, it was not surprising that the couple chose to get married in that special house on California Drive. However, some quick work was needed. The house needed painting inside and out. As usual, Clinton had no trouble enlisting his friends to help fix up the future homestead before the wedding date.

On 7 p.m. the night of Saturday, October 11, 1975, Bill Clinton married Hillary Rodham while their families and close friends looked on. The couple exchanged family heirloom rings as part of their vows. On the following days, hundreds of wellwishers flocked to the Fayetteville house. Clinton used the opportunity to announce his plans to run for election in 1976. He did not know whether he wanted to go after Hammerschmidt's congressional slot again or to run for the state's attorney general's spot. Whatever the case, Bill Clinton was ready to make another run for office, and he could hardly wait to hit the campaign trail.

Chapter 4
A Taste of Power

O n April 1, 1976, William Jefferson Clinton officially filed papers as a candidate for Attorney General of Arkansas–and it was certainly no April Fool's joke. This time he was determined to win. There was a three-man race in the Democratic primary, with Clinton facing George T. Jernigan, a former secretary of state and Clarence Cash, an assistant attorney general. Because of Clinton's recent race against Hammerschmidt, most of the Arkansas voters knew where the thirty-year-old law professor stood. He ran away with the election, capturing over 60 per cent of the vote. Recognizing Clinton's strength, the Republicans did not even bother running a candidate against him in the November contest.

Bill went right to work as soon as he took office in January of 1977. He had picked up some valuable tips from his predecessor, Jim Guy Tucker, who had already acknowledged that Clinton was "very bright and capable of understanding what you can and cannot do with the law." The new attorney general put together a staff young in age and idealistic in philosophy. "Your legs had to keep up with your mind or vice versa," observed one assistant, "and we all have to do double-time in both areas to keep up with the boss."

Doing Battle

As soon as he settled into office, Clinton began doing

battle. The business and political establishment of Arkansas stood firmly in place, dominated by individuals long accustomed to running the state legislature. Utilities held special power, raising and lowering rates as they wished. No more of that, Bill Clinton decided, and he pushed for tighter restrictions over rate increases. Immediately, he was called as a consumer advocate, looking after the average Arkansas taxpayer. In order to alleviate the overcrowded conditions in the state's prisons, the new attorney general streamlined and expanded the work release program for prisoners. During the day, they worked at regular jobs. At night, they were locked up. Clinton hoped the program would better prepare the offenders for life after confinement.

Clinton enjoyed his work as attorney general, even thrived on it. He took his message to the people, accepting speaking engagements like no other attorney general had done before. He found much fulfillment in working for the people of Arkansas. Yet there was more he wanted to do. As the end of his two year term approached, he began to think of other ways of helping his state. People talked to him of seeking the governor's position or a United States Senate seat. By the end of 1977, Clinton had made his decision. He would go after the governor's post.

Into the Governor's Race

Clinton's past experiences with both national and state office seeking proved beneficial in setting up his campaign for governor. "Every voter counts," Clinton told his political helpers. "We do not cater to groups; we care about individuals. Be willing to listen."

In the Democratic primary held early in 1978, Clinton faced four candidates. Joe D. Woodward and Clinton proved the top vote votegetters. In a run-off election, the former attorney general coasted to an easy win, pulling in almost 60 per cent of the vote.

Republican state chairman Lynn Lowe was Clinton's opponent in the November contest. Staunchly identified as an advocate of educational reform, the former attorney general promoted the importance of young people as the major factor in Arkansas's future. "If our boys and girls do not get a quality education in this state, we will never have a firm and solid economic base," Clinton declared. "Our future is in the hands of the young."

Among Clinton's biggest supporters were the teachers, who applauded their candidate's efforts to increase salaries in education. "Our teachers are the poorest paid and hardest working in the nation," the candidate asserted.

Whereas most political candidates tired quickly from the endless campaigning required in seeking a major office, Bill Clinton seemed rejuvenated. Said writer David Osborne, "Clinton thrives on the handshaking and elbow-rubbing that are the backbone of politics in Arkansas, and people bask in his warmth."

ANSWERING HIS CRITICS

Not that Clinton did not have his attackers and critics. Some found his youth (he was only thirty-one) unacceptable, feeling that a more mature leader was needed to head the state government. Clinton's views, whether they be on matters of gun control, abortion, capital punishment, or marijuana legislation, were considered too liberal by many Arkansas residents. Some people took exception to Hillary's continued use of her own last name. And there were those who felt that Clinton was merely using the governor's slot as a stepping-stone toward higher office.

"I would serve as governor of this state as long as the people would have me," Clinton told a group of high-school journalists. "I want the chance to push this state forward, to make it outstanding in every possible way." The voters of Arkansas offered Clinton the chance. They gave him a landslide victory over Lowe, 338,684 to 195,550.

Speculations Grow

No sooner had Clinton captured the governorship when speculations began about him becoming a national candidate for vice-president. After all, he had run a smooth statewide organization for Jimmy Carter when he sought the top office. Now that he was in the White House, there were rumors he might wish to bump Walter Mondale out as vice-president.

Then there was Senator Edward Kennedy of Massachusetts. Some Democrats were urging the last of the famed Kennedy brothers to run for the presidency. Ever since a tragic accident in 1969 in which Kennedy was driving and a young secretary was killed, the senator had shied away from the top office. But now there was talk of him trying for the position. If he did so he would need a running mate. Clinton was a distinct possibility. "I appreciate the attention," Clinton mused, "but I'd just like to have a chance to do the job I was elected to do."

TAKING THE OATH

On January 9, 1979, William Jefferson Clinton took the oath of office as Governor of Arkansas. As his wife Hillary held the Bible, a jammed chamber of the House of Representatives looked on. In his inaugural address, the youngest governor in the United States pledged to pursue a program of quality education for all children in the state, protection of the environment, tax relief for the elderly, and equal opportunity for all, regardless of age, sex, religion or color.

The people of Arkansas soon learned that their new governor was not merely a man of words without action. Education came first, and it came with many reforms. A $1,200 salary increase for teachers was included in the first Clinton budget. He wanted all teachers to take the national teachers' exam before being certified to teach in Arkansas, and he wanted a statewide student testing program in the basic subject areas. "We want the best to be behind the big desks and the best to be sitting in the smaller desks," he declared. As a special program to reach gifted students Clinton proposed a streamlined summer school session. Most of Clinton's initial educational programs won wide support, however one of his efforts fell flat. He wanted smaller school districts to consolidate and form larger districts that could offer more services at less cost. The legislators wanted none of such a change.

Neither was the "car tag fee" well received. Hoping to repair Arkansas highways, Clinton pushed through a law that raised motor vehicle registration charges. Many of the consumers that the recently installed governor had promised to protect objected, feeling he had double-crossed them. "We will remember this," one taxpayer promised.

Welcome, Chelsea!

Summer of 1979 brought exciting news to the Clinton family. Hillary was expecting a baby. The delighted couple took a course in the Lamaze method of delivery, but they did not get a chance to use their skills. Due to arrive in the middle of March, Chelsea Victoria Clinton made her appearance on February 27, 1980, some two weeks early. The baby was delivered by cesarean section in the Little Rock Baptist Medical Center. The proud father spent the rest of the night walking the halls, his new daughter held carefully in his arms. "It was something my own father did not get to do," commented Clinton.

But the duties of the governorship demanded Clinton's

constant attention, and he was always looking ahead. As Clinton's two year term drew to a close, a primary battle loomed. He took on a 77-year-old farmer named Monroe Schwarzlose, who won a surprising 31 per cent of the vote. Clearly, Clinton was vulnerable. However, the Republican challenger, Frank White, was given little chance of beating the incumbent.

CUBANS CAUSE TROUBLE

Enter Fidel Castro. The communist leader of Cuba suddenly allowed 120,000 "undesirables" to leave the country. Seeking the security of the United States, the Cubans boarded anything that could float and sailed west. When this tidal wave of Cubans poured into the United States seeking safety and security, President Jimmy Carter had to act fast. Federal army bases, including Arkansas's Fort Chaffee, were turned into housing units for the refugees.

Of the 20,000 Cubans housed at Fort Chaffee, many expected to find comfort and cleanliness. The tales of grand and gracious living in the United States had attracted countless refugees to the American shores. But the conditions were not what was expected. Food was rationed and living space was scarce. Fights broke out inside the fort, and on May 26, more than three hundred of the refugees broke out of the fort itself. They raced into the countryside, sending panic and fear among Arkansas citizens.

Governor Clinton did not waste a second. He called out the Arkansas National Guard, ordering them to protect the people. Police officers were put on extra shifts, and in less than seventy-two hours, the Cubans were arrested.

The quiet did not last long. On June 1, more trouble exploded. Fighting broke out inside the fort, and again refugees charged the gate and knocked down barricades. Two hundred Cubans raced down Highway 22, heading toward the town of

Barling near Fort Smith. By the time the mob arrived on the outskirts of Barling, the policemen were waiting. Armed with guns and nightsticks, the officers arrested the Cubans, but not before five of them were shot.

Despite Clinton's quick and forceful actions during the Fort Chaffee riots, the people of Arkansas felt he should have stood up to President Carter, demanding the chief executive keep better control over federal troops. "This was not a state problem, it was a problem for the federal government," wrote one newspaper editor. "Clinton should not have allowed all these refugees into the state. When the trouble started, he should have demanded more immediate response."

Counting the Ballots

The Republican challenger, White, hurled angry criticism at the governor, accusing him of waiting too long and not exercising the powers of his office during the Cuban situation. White also insisted Clinton had not inspired the job growth and development he had promised. Still annoyed by Clinton's stand on rate increases, the utility companies threw their support behind White.

As usual, the Democratic machinery was in place under Clinton efficient direction. Yet he had uneasy feelings as election day approached. And his political sense was right on target. For the second time in his political career, Bill Clinton lost. Of 840,000 votes, Clinton fell short by some 35,000 ballots. The youngest governor in the nation now became the nation's youngest ex-governor.

"The people have spoken," Clinton declared. "I cannot say it does not hurt to lose, but this is the system under which our government operates, and it is a fair system indeed." Bill Clinton left the governor's mansion a sad but wiser man. Most people knew for certain that his political career was far from over.

Chapter 5

Making A Comeback

Although Bill Clinton missed the day-to-day excitement of political life, he welcomed the opportunity to spend more time with his family. When a chance came to travel abroad with a church group, Hillary and Bill signed up. It was a memorable trip to Israel, where they visited Jerusalem, Galilee, and Masada. The trip offered a chance to enjoy the favorite tourist attractions, soak up fascinating political history, and gain new energy for the future.

Upon his return to America, Clinton pondered a run for the chairmanship of the Democratic National Party. After some deliberation, he turned the idea down. Instead, he accepted a job with the law firm of Wright Lindsey & Jennings in Little Rock. He was considered an expert in the area of business and commercial litigation. Certainly, having a former Arkansas governor as a member of the firm provided added prestige.

Waiting and Watching

But while Clinton handled his legal matters, he also watched the way Frank White handled the governorship. White seemed to leap ineffectively from one problem area to another, managing to annoy or offend many Arkansas citizens. He permitted the utility companies to raise their rates, putting a tight squeeze on many state residents, especially the elderly. He signed a bill into law allowing the teaching of "Creation Science." When the bill was declared unconstitutional, White admitted he had not even read the bill. For a person who had risen to the top political office in the state largely through his criticism of his predecessor, the governor seemed determined to make even more political blunders himself. Some called White "Governor Goofy."

Beginning in the summer of 1981, Clinton took to the Arkansas roads, traveling to city and country, talking to people. He carried a two-fold message: "I'm sorry for not listening to your problems, and I'll do better the next time."

Being a Listener

Early in 1981, Clinton was ready to go public with a formal announcement of his plans to run for governor again. "You can't lead without listening," Clinton told his television and radio audience. He explained how he had spent the last six months listening, and now he felt equipped to lead, if they would give him a chance.

As the campaign heated up, the mudslinging turned ugly. White's supporters depicted Clinton as an East Coast Ivy Leaguer with liberal beliefs. Clinton's backers counter-attacked with White portrayed as an underhanded sneak who tried to please everyone to sought his favor.

Few of Bill Clinton's campaigners were as effective as his wife. Dumping the name Hillary Rodham, she emerged as Hillary Clinton and hit the speaking trail full blast. The Arkansas Gazette declared that "Mrs. Clinton is almost certainly the best speaker among politicians' wives, probably the only one who can fully engage an audience on her own merits, rather than just as somebody's wife."

The Polls Open

Despite Frank White's ineptitude as governor, Clinton

knew that defeating the incumbent would be a tough task. As election day approached, the former governor got even rougher with his criticisms. Clinton berated White for firing top quality people in the state government, while hammering at the increase in utility taxes. "He raises prices of medicine for Medicaid recipients, and yet gives tax breaks to major corporations," Clinton charged.

The more Clinton spoke publicly, the more polished and professional he sounded. As an astute political move, the candidate scheduled a last-minute message to the voters. He appeared on a special television broadcast on the Saturday night before Tuesday's selection. With smooth delivery and careful details, he laid out his plans for the governorship.

When the Arkansas voters cast their ballots, Clinton again made history. He became the first ex-governor to win back the top statehouse spot, capturing 54.7 percent of the vote.

ANOTHER CHANCE

In January of 1983, William Jefferson Clinton offered his second inauguration speech after swearing-in ceremonies. He outlined a program with a double "E" focus–education and economics. Recognizing his wife's following among the state's citizens, he named her as head of the Arkansas Education Standards Committee.

Hillary Clinton went right to work, traveling the state, holding hearings and meeting with teachers and parents. She put together a blueprint for educational improvements. The plan called for reducing class size, increasing accountability, and meeting the needs of all children. As soon as her husband had the proposals in his hands, Clinton pushed for a tax increase to improve education funding. Legislators agreed, on one condition–teachers had to pass a basic skills test to be certified. The state education association vehemently opposed the condition, but Clinton refused to give in. "We want the best to teach our kids!" he declared.

There was no doubt what kind of forum Bill Clinton most enjoyed as a politician. To many people, the town meeting was a thing of the past, an outdated manner of bringing local people together to hear their complaints and ideas. But Bill Clinton thrived on such give and take, often arming himself with a notepad and jotting down what people had to say. "He listens," more than one person declared. "He cares what we have to say."

TARGETING EDUCATION

Education remained Clinton's primary target for reform. Again and again he insisted that unless drastic changes took place in the Arkansas educational program, nothing else could get better. He called on legislators in their offices and called them on the phone at all hours. By late 1983, Clinton got the results he wanted. The Arkansas State Legislature passed tax increases that would lead to improved education policies. "I thank you," Clinton told the government officials, "Arkansas thanks you, but most important of all, the kids of this state thank you."

There was no doubt that Clinton had learned much since his first stint as governor. Always a skilled speaker, his ability to do a quick study of a bill, capture the essential features, and summarize the most complicated language into layman's terms became a constant source of conversation around the state's capitol. In Washington, D. C., the Republicans had shoved Jimmy Carter out of the presidency and put Ronald Reagan in his place. Often Clinton's ability to communicate was compared with Reagan's, with his supporters adding that Clinton had not spent a lifetime as an actor rehearsing lines. As the early months of 1984 slipped by, Clinton's name was bandied around as a possible vice-presidential candidate for the Democrats. Clearly, however, the Arkansas governor liked the job he held.

A SAD SURPRISE

Overall, the people of the state also seemed to like the job Clinton was doing. He seemed certain for re-election to another two year term. His work to revolutionize education captured national attention, however he sometimes had trouble with state's teacher unions. Nonetheless, his approval ratings were high. Then, in May, came a stunning surprise that hit the governor hard. A call arrived from Colonel Tommy Goodwin, head of the Arkansas State Police. Bill Clinton's younger brother, Roger, was accused of using and trafficking cocaine.

"What do you want us to do?" Goodwin asked.

"Do what you have to do," the governor replied sadly.

The next weeks were a constant nightmare for Bill Clinton. Desperately he wanted to believe his brother was innocent, that some mistake had been made. But the evidence was overwhelming. Clinton and his wife read everything they could find about drug addiction. Maybe they could find some way of reaching out, of helping.

Yet the information Bill Clinton had received was confidential. The investigation was ongoing. Hopefully, Roger might cut himself off from his involvement with drugs, a habit that had grown into a four-gram-a-day addiction.

Under Arrest

It was not to be. In August, three months after that initial telephone call from Goodwin, Roger Clinton was arrested in Hot Springs. It was revealed he had been abusing drugs for the past thirteen years. He was now twenty-eight, and if he had not been in such good physical shape, doctors claimed he would have died with such a heavy drug intake.

"This is a time of great pain and sadness for me and my family," Governor Clinton declared in a public statement. "My brother has apparently become involved with drugs, a curse which has reached epidemic proportions and has plagued the lives of millions of families in our nation, including many in our own state. I ask for the prayers of our family at this difficult time for my brother, for my family, and for me. I love my brother very much and will be of comfort to him, but I want his case to be handled exactly as any other similar case would be."

People followed the Clinton case through the media. At first, Roger Clinton denied he was a drug addict. Bill Clinton would not accept that denial, insisting that if Roger were not an addict, his punishment should be even more harsh for "putting cocaine into the bodies of others for money." By November, Roger Clinton had changed his innocent plea to guilty on two drug related charges. On the first charge, he received a suspended three-year sentence, but on the second charge, he was sentenced to two years in prison.

"I accept the judgment of the court with respect," announced Bill Clinton, after his brother's sentencing. "Now all of us in my brother's family must do everything we can to help him free himself of his drug dependency. I hope the publicity this case received will discourage other young people from involvement with drugs and will increase public awareness of the staggering dimensions of the drug problem in our state and nation. I am more deeply committed than ever before to do all that I can to fight against illegal drugs and to prevent other families from experiencing the personal tragedy and pain drug abuse has brought to us."

The entire affair was personally agonizing for Bill Clinton. He knew Roger was angry that although his own brother was governor, he had not exerted any influence to help. Other family members had struggled with the problem too. Politically, it was impossible to know how the incident would affect Clinton's chances on election day in November. Despite the overall success of his educational reforms within the state, the Arkansas Education Association still resented Clinton's insistence on teacher testing to gain creditation. Since this was a presidential election year, there was concern that the immensely popular Republican Reagan would help pull in many state Republican office-seekers on his coattails.

Going to the Polls

When the voters went to the polls, their feelings became clear. Clinton again won the governorship with 554,561 votes against the Republican challenger, Woody Freeman, who garnered 331,987. Roger Clinton's drug problem, rather than being a major negative factor, proved to have little effect on the election. Perhaps many people sympathized with Bill Clinton's problem. As he had said openly, drugs had brought trouble and turmoil in homes everywhere. He had let the system of justice operate without any outside pressure. Not only did the voters return Clinton to the governor's job, they passed a state constitutional amendment lengthening the term from two years to four years, effective in 1986.

For the third time, William Jefferson Clinton took the oath of office as governor of the state of Arkansas. In his inaugural address of January, 1985, he promised to focus on job growth within the state just as he had pushed educational reform. "Our administration will pursue an ambitious agenda for Arkansas's future," proclaimed the governor, "an agenda based on our commitment to economic growth, our commitment to excellence in education and our commitment to increased security and stability for our people."

Testing the Teachers

That "commitment to excellence in education" included plans for statewide testing the teachers. The formidable Arkansas Education Association had opposed that idea from its first public mention. Now, the organization of teachers prepared to do battle. Teacher leaders threatened to boycott the testing. It was clear that teachers were not the only individuals thrown into a testing situation. Governor Bill Clinton was being tested too.

Chapter 6

"That Fellow from Arkansas"

Both Bill and Hillary Clinton could not understand the reluctance of the Arkansas Education Association in supporting teacher testing. "A major reason for higher educational standards," insisted Hillary Clinton, "is to provide a better-educated work force in Arkansas so we can be more competitive for jobs. We have a long way to go to convince ourselves as well as people outside of Arkansas, that our citizens are educated to the point that will enable them to compete with workers from not just around the country, but around the world." It seemed clear to her that to have better educated students, you had to have qualified teachers.

Opposition from teachers stemmed from a feeling that they were the lowest-paid teachers in the entire country and yet they had to be tested to hold down those jobs. In states paying double the salaries Arkansas teachers received, no tests were required.

Public support for teacher testing slowly gathered support, yet the teachers stood firm in their opposition. "No one test should determine a person's competency to do a job," declared one AEA official. "As teachers, we do not pass or fail our students on the basis of one test."

Back and forth the conflict continued, to the point that Hillary Clinton referred to her husband and herself as "combat veterans" on the issue.

Passing the Test

Statewide testing was scheduled for March 23, 1985. Arkansas Education Association leaders threatened to boycott testing locations. What would be the state's reaction to that?

The question proved to be academic. On the assigned testing date, 25,077 teachers took the nation's first basic skills test. There were widespread rumors that the test had been leaked to the educators in advance, to avoid anyone failing the exam. Not so, declared the Arkansas Department of Education. The test was held to be valid and uncompromised.

In the next year, teachers who failed the test were allowed to take it again–and again and again–as many times as it took to pass. Each time, some 10 per cent of those taking the test failed. When the statewide testing program of teachers was done, 1,315 had not passed and were forced to leave teaching because of low test scores. That represented 3.5 per cent of teachers in Arkansas. However, there were also teachers who left the teaching profession rather than take the required test.

Lifting the Economy

Although much of his attention had been focused on educational improvements, Clinton recognized the need to attend to other matters too. He spearheaded a plan which offered tax-exempt bonds that would encourage new industries and jobs within Arkansas. He also provided incentives for the state's major pension funds to be invested. Clinton's moves caused those who had criticized him for being too focused on education to re-evaluate the governor. He came out of the evaluation as a decent businessman.

Speeding Up "Due Process"

For some time, those charged with crimes in the state

spent many months, even years, before being brought to trial. Not only was the delay difficult to the accused, it was expensive to the state to provide food and housing for those held for trial. "Worst of all," Clinton noted, "is the hardship placed upon the victims of the accused, who must stand ready to appear and testify at any time. These innocent people need to get on with their lives." Through Clinton's leadership, laws were passed aimed at protecting the rights of victims of crimes, and requiring trials to be held within nine months of indictment.

Conscience and Controversy

The controversial issue of abortion raised its head during the 1985 session of the Arkansas State Legislature. Clinton wrestled with his personal convictions in the matter. He knew that if he planned an extended political career–and it was becoming more and more apparent that he did–his thinking would be held up to public examination. A longtime Baptist, Clinton turned to the Biblical Scripture and clergy to help crystallize his thinking. He resolved that life began at birth, therefore he felt comfortable signing a bill that came out of the legislature prohibiting abortions after the twenty-fifth week of pregnancy and prohibiting the abortion of fetuses which could survive outside the womb. It put him in the camp of the those who felt the woman had the right to choose, and lost him support among pro-life factions.

GAINING STAR STATUS

By the middle of 1985, there was little doubt the National Democratic Committee saw Governor Bill Clinton of Arkansas as a political star on the rise. Ever since being elected to the state's top office the first time, he was a contender. But his defeat after only one term made some believe he might be merely a flash in the pan. Not so any more. His solid stance on educational and economic concerns and his subsequent programs to deal with them, as well as his direct dealings with controversial matters, gave him added stature. "That fellow from Arkansas bears watching," observed more than one political analyst. Clinton, too, was thinking beyond the governor's mansion in Little Rock. As far as a bid for the presidency, he told a reporter from the Atlantic Constitution in May of 1985, "It would be fun to run, even if you lost. It would be a challenge to go out and meet the people and try to communicate your ideas and bring the different parts of the country together."

Yet Clinton seemed to becoming more and more comfortable sitting in the Arkansas governor's chair. He was elected chairman of the Southern Growth Policies Board and vice-chairman of the National Governors Association. In such positions, he constantly demonstrated a talent for compromise and mediation. "Our main interest is people," he asserted often. "We cannot ever forget when we are talking about industry or education or whatever, we are talking about people, their wishes and their needs."

Late in 1985, Clinton captained a delegation of trade representatives on a trip to Japan. Always an enthusiastic cheerleader for his home state, he won quick friends and warm receptions wherever he went. By the time he returned to the United States, Clinton could claim a number of new economic ties between Arkansas and Japan.

Making Welfare Fair

Creating new business opportunities was exciting, yet Clinton and other government leaders recognized the need for taking a careful look at the welfare system at both and national and state levels. During the summer of 1986, Clinton tackled the problem as co-chairman of the National Governors Association Task Force on Welfare Reform. To Clinton, the solution to the problem was relatively simple. "Working Americans are far happier than out-of-work Americans," he declared. "The country is must stronger too. Welfare programs are job programs."

Not one to talk without doing, Clinton rolled his philosophy into action, establishing a job/welfare program in Arkansas. In less than five years, more than two hundred people were moving from welfare rolls into the work force every month. National leaders hailed Clinton's energy and progressive momentum.

Seeking Another Term

Clinton announced early that he would seek a fourth term as Governor of Arkansas in 1986, and few opponents jumped forward to challenge him. He was riding a popularity seldom achieved in state. His election was a foregone conclusion. His impact on education and the economy in Arkansas was obvious.

In August, the National Governors Association elected Bill Clinton their chairman. He appealed to his counterparts to reach out to the people within their respective states, emphasizing that people who were working and productive were the nation's greatest strength.

To no one's surprise, Clinton swept to a landslide victory in November's election, capturing 64 per cent of the vote. Arkansas was observing its 150th year as a state, and Clinton forecast that the best years were still ahead. Speaking as much as a father figure than as a governor, he told the people "It's time for all of us to pull together as a family."

Emphasizing the Economy

Facing a budget shortfall, Clinton took immediate action to boost the economy. He wanted to avoid a tax increase, especially right after assuming his new term in office. Such a

Candidate Clinton emerges from the voting booth with six-year-old Chelsea after casting his vote in the Democratic primary in 1986. He won the primary contest, and then went on to win re-election to the governor's spot. (Associated Press)

move would hardly seem an affirmation of his past planning, nor would it send a heartening message to voters who had just showed their confidence in him. Carefully he proposed a state tax code more closely resembling the federal income tax structure. The plan hit a snag in the Arkansas House of Representatives, but with tinkering, a compromise proposal passed.

Clinton's educational reforms, won admiration within Arkansas and other states, but they demanded more funding. Appeals to the federal government found few listeners in Washington. The philosophy of President Ronald Reagan was "Less government is better government." It fell to the state and municipalities to raise their own funds locally to cover their expenses. As a result, Clinton had little choice but to seek occasional tax increases. Nonetheless, Arkansas consistently remained among those states with the lowest per-capita tax burdens.

Into the Major Leagues

By the time talk became more serious about possible Democrats to seek the 1988 top ticket slot, Bill Clinton's name was bandied about in many of the higher echelons. After all, he had proven his vote getting power in having won four consecutive terms as Governor of Arkansas. His reforms as the state's chief executive were being praised and imitated across the country. Articulate and dynamic, he was handsome as well–certainly a positive factor where the media was concerned. More and more often, Clinton was asked the question: "Would you consider being a candidate for President of the United States?" His lips curved into a grin and his eyes brightened. "It's an interesting thought," he answered. "It's worth thinking about."

Chapter 7

To Run–Or Not to Run

No doubt countless hours went into the decision-making process for Bill Clinton. Politics flowed through his veins, and the thought of making a run for the nation's top office was indeed attractive. After all, Jimmy Carter had stepped from a governor's chair into the presidential seat. Bill Clinton wondered if he could do the same.

And yet there were other points to consider. At forty-two, he was still a "golden boy" of the Democratic Party. Certainly, many leaders cast respectful glances in his direction, yet there were those who felt he still had time before making "the big run."

For Bill Clinton himself, there were personal considerations. His wife was a valuable teammate, not just a companion on the campaign trail but a bright co-worker. Hillary enjoyed politics, but even more she thrived on causes related to the well being of children. She could–and would–lend strength and moral support to a presidential campaign.

Considering Everyone

Yet both Bill and Hillary felt a presidential bid would be a tremendous strain on young Chelsea. At eight, she was a lively, well-adjusted, carefree child. How would months and months of being under media scrutiny, separated often from one or both parents, affect the girl? Neither of her parents wanted to find out. There would be no bid for the presidency in 1988.

However, although the door might be temporarily closed, it would not be permanently locked. Clinton made it known that he was available for whatever tasks the National Democratic Party might have for him, the more visible to the public, the better.

Gaining More Exposure

In the summer of 1988, Bill Clinton got a chance for major national exposure. The Democrats convened in Atlanta to nominated their presidential and vice-presidential candidates. When the delegates gave the top slot to Governor Michael Dukakis of Massachusetts, Clinton was tapped to give one of the nominating speeches. He jumped at the chance.

From his high school days, Clinton had perfected his own style of formal public speaking. With a few key notes and select phrases, he could bring a crowd to life. But Dukakis advisors would not allow Clinton that kind of freedom. They prepared their own speech of nomination, insisting that Clinton stick to their text.

A Speech Without an End

No one had a better sense of how well a speech was capturing a crowd's attention and enthusiasm than Bill Clinton. If only he could share his own words and not have to read from a Teleprompter, he knew could do the job right. Yet the Dukakis people wanted it done their way–and Bill Clinton was a team player. As he stood at the podium, droning on and on about the merits of Michael Dukakis, he had a sudden urge to wrap up the speech early. No, he resisted the urge and continued on–and on and on. For thirty-three minutes Clinton spoke. Finally, when he said "In conclusion..." the crowd applauded. The nominator could not wait to sit down.

Television and radio commentators could not help but criticize Clinton's nominating speech. "It was clearly the case of a soldier following the orders of his commanding generals," observed Dan Rather of CBS. In the days that followed, newspapers also noted the Arkansas governor's lengthy address, but thankfully, it became a lighthearted joke rather that any brutal attack. Clearly, the media liked Bill Clinton, and those on the inside of the political world knew he was just doing his job.

Bouncing Back

Clinton, himself, bounced back. As a guest on Johnny Carson's "Tonight Show," the Arkansas governor was introduced as "an over the counter sleep aid." The jovial television host also referred to Clinton as "a windbag." Some politicians might have been insulted. Not Clinton. He went along with each gag, adding a few quips of his own. Then he delighted the audience by playing his saxophone. With the backup of Doc Severinsen's band, the strains of "Summertime" glided gracefully over the television airwaves. "Being long-winded isn't always a weakness," the Arkansas governor wisecracked. "It helps when playing an instrument." The people watching and listening loved the presentation. Memories of the Dukakis nominating speech faded quickly from people's minds, replaced instead by the image of an energetic, charismatic young man from Arkansas who knew how to laugh at himself and relax before millions of "Tonight" fans.

But Clinton took his full-time job as governor seriously, constantly trying to find new ways of building his state's economy and treasury. When he heard of a state developing a fresh industry or product, he investigated personally or through his staff. "It must benefit the people," he insisted. "Arkansas doesn't need something that only makes a couple people rich.

It needs businesses that give people jobs."

Helping the Young

Children also received Clinton's consistent focus. Whether it be their education or medical health, the Arkansas governor sought means for offering a stabilizing direction to their years of growing up. The National Women's Political Caucus named him as one of their annual "Good Guys," citing his continuous and widespread advocacy of child care.

Such recognition seemed to spur Clinton on. In December of 1988, he proposed that financial assistance and medicaid for two parent families, on the condition that one parent remain in the home six months out of the year and that both parents participate in an education, training, and work programs. Single-parent families were not overlooked. The governor sought child care and medical coverage, allowing the parent to work during the day. Absentee parents, behind in child support payments, should have such debts withheld for their paychecks, Clinton argued.

Establishing "Boot Camps"

While government officials across the nation searched for a means to cut down on juvenile criminals, Clinton signed into law a bill establishing "boot camps" for first-time offenders, many of them young delinquents. Rather than going to jail, those found guilty of serious criminal offenses headed to camps where strict discipline, rehabilitation, and training programs were implemented.

EVALUATING EDUCATION

While attending to a multitude of state problems, Clinton still remained focused on the importance of education. Within the Arkansas Department of Education, he established an internal division known as the Office of Accountability. The latter office was given the power to evaluate local educational systems and to issue report card grades on their performance. College teachers were also graded. "Someone must have told our distinguished governor that his primary role was to act as an educational headmaster," observed more than one skeptic. Yet most people praised Clinton for his bold and dramatic steps to bring Arkansas into the spotlight of progress in education.

In January of 1989, George Bush took over the presidential duties from Ronald Reagan. Although he was in the other major political party, Clinton was still called upon for a major leadership role. At a national summit meeting held in Charlottesville, Virginia, the governor of Arkansas took an active role in formulating educational goals for the entire country.

Caring for the Children

While her husband carried out his duties, Hillary Clinton raised her own voice about a nagging concern. Yes, educating the youth of America was important. But it was even more important that those boys and girls live beyond infancy. Bending President Bush's ear at a luncheon, Hillary Clinton urged the chief executive to investigate the present statistics regarding children's health in the nation. President Bush did exactly that, and conceded that there was indeed a problem.

As Clinton's fourth term drew to a close, he could look back on a variety of accomplishments. The Arkansas governor could claim top grades to educational and health reform, improvements in the system of criminal justice, and some headway in economic programs. Perhaps his greatest frustration with the Arkansas legislature was its unwillingness to fund pay increases for teachers, college faculty and state employees.

MAKING HISTORY

No person had ever sought a fifth term as governor of the state of Arkansas. Would Bill Clinton? The speculation began early in 1990, and continued to gain momentum. In March, the 43-year-old man from Hope announced his plans to do just that. The passion for the job had dimmed a bit, and Clinton admitted that "the fire of an election no longer burns in me." Despite that feeling, he declared that he "still didn't want to stop doing the job."

John Brummett, a reporter for the Arkansas *Gazette,* took heated exception to Clinton's remarks. Over the years, the independent *Gazette,* home-based in Little Rock, had been a frequent ally of the governor's, supporting many of his projects and reforms. Not that the influential newspaper could not hurl criticism as well. But overall, the *Gazette* was a Clinton backer. One of the *Gazette's* top columnists, Brummett was a close observer of the governor, ready to toss bouquets or grenades as the situation seemed to warrant. When Clinton announced his plan to run for an unprecedented fifth term, Brummett took a feisty stand, admitting that Clinton's remarks were "candid, sane and human." The columnist suggested that Clinton might have been in office too long and suffered from "burnout." Brummett also resented Clinton's idea that he really didn't want to campaign again, but would "do the people the kind favor of staying on the job."

Rumors or Reality?

If the sparks ignited by Clinton's word choice on announcing his fifth candidacy were not enough, speculation about his sex life added to the fire. A former state employee, Larry Nichols, who had been fired from his state job filed suit against the Arkansas governor. Nichols accused Clinton of carrying on affairs with five women while in office. One of these women, Gennifer Flowers, fanned the flames. The woman vehemently denied the accusations, yet in choosing to do so she became a part of the media spotlight. Most of the media viewed Nichols as a man with a grudge for losing his state job, but more than a few eyebrows were lifted in Arkansas. Clinton's good looks and charms made the charges seem all the more possible, if not probable.

Another facet of Clinton's personal life popped up regarding the Arkansas governor's use of drugs. One of Clinton's potential Republican challengers was a man named Tommy Robinson, who was known to have battled with a drinking problem. It seemed only fair that Clinton reveal any history he had with drugs. This time it was John Brummett who championed Clinton's side. "What matters is that he does not use drugs now, and has not for at least a very long time. For twelve years in the public eye he has shown himself to be in constantly sober control of his mental and physical faculties." As for the past, in Clinton's pre-governor days, Brummett suggested that "as a lad or college student — drug use was prevalent among people of his age and station in life, and on one or a few occasion he inhaled from what was commonly called a joint." Although he didn't know it, Brummett was right on target, according to a later admission by Clinton.

Seeking Other Offices

During his previous four terms as governor of Arkansas, Clinton had become a national figure politically. Some wondered if he might be tempted to give up the job if he were elected, so that he could reach for higher office in the nation. One newsman, Craig Canoon, put the question directly to Clinton: "Will you guarantee all of us that if reelected, there is absolutely, positively no way that you'll run for any other political office and that you'll serve out your full term?" There was no hesitation from Clinton. "You bet. I told you when I announced for governor that I intended to run, and that's what

Taking the Heat

"If you can't stand the heat, stay out of the kitchen."
Harry Truman's advice to those seeking the top
politicial office was just one of the thirty-third
President's wise maxims. Truman recognized to be
the chief executive of the United States carries enor-
mous responsibility, and there will always be those
who criticize a President's actions and decisions.
According to Truman, if one cannot accept criticism,
that person has no business occupying the country's
top office.

In a nip and tuck election battle in the fall of 1992,
Bill Clinton squeezed out a narrow victory over
George Bush and Ross Perot. Clinton's 43% popular
vote tally left him open and vulnerable to attacks from
critics even before he took office in January of 1993.

Among the most vocal of Clinton adversaries became radio and television commentator and best
selling author Rush Limbaugh. Labeling himself a
"conservative" and declaring the Republicans more in
tune with conservative ideology than the Democrats,
Limbaugh immediately championed a strong bloc of
citizens regularly critical of Clinton and any others
supporting or even somewhat appreciating "liberal"
philosophies. Usually deaf to Limbaugh criticisms,
Clinton took to the airwaves himself during the summer of 1994, claiming Limbaugh enjoyed hours of
media time each day in order to attack the Clinton
administration. As President, offering a weekly brief
radio message, he had little opportunity to respond to
the constant Limbaugh plummeting. If Clinton had
hoped Limbaugh might let up a bit, the nation's top
elected official was totally wrong. The Presidential
outburst seemed only to make matters worse, as
Limbaugh used Clinton's attitude as one more target
for attack.

Political cartooning has also enjoyed a longtime
existance as a means for leveling Presidential criti-

cism. Usually such drawings are found on the editorial pages of newspapers and magazines, but one popular artist achieved a style that allows his depictions to appear anywhere in print. Garry Trudeau seems to play no favorites politically. During the Republican administration of President George Bush, the chief executive was represented simply by open space that could speak, suggesting there was nothing much there as a leader. Bush's vice-president, Dan Quayle, was drawn as a talking feather, representing a true lightweight of little substance. Initially, Clinton appeared to enjoy more favor in the political pen of Trudeau, until the cartoonist felt the President displayed indecision once too often. Suddenly a flying waffle began appearing in print, reflecting Clinton's inability to make policies and stick with them. Word quickly circulated around the White House that Trudeau was no longer held in favor. The cartoonist seemed little affected by the change in Clinton's attitude, and the newspaper panels continued to poke fun at the commander-in-chief.

"A President has to have a thick skin," Harry Truman said once while being criticized for firing the military hero Douglas MacArthur. "Too bad we can't be fitted for a layer of elephant hide upon being elected."

I'm gonna do. I'm gonna run for four years. I made that decision when I decided to run. I'm being considered as a candidate for governor. That's the job I want. That's the job I'll do for the next four years."

Despite the devoted supporters Clinton had lined up in the past, he faced considerable opposition in both the Democratic primary, and, if he won that, in the final election against a Republican opponent. State legislators were weary of his efforts to increase school financing since they required tax increases. Labor union leaders and members were angry at the Clinton administration for extending a big loan to a company in the midst of a negotiations dispute. Teachers were tired of his demand for competency tests. Although he seemed to have worked hard to build the state's economy and push through educational reform, critics felt Clinton "had done it his way without seeking the wisdom of those who understood the situation better."

Some of the people of Arkansas also felt that Hillary Clinton was too big a public presence. Not content to play the campaigner's wife, smiling and waving on cue, the outspoken Mrs. Clinton was perfectly happy taking the podium herself, eloquently and forcefully explaining the past, present, and future programs of her husband's administration. When asked about his wife's activities, Bill Clinton just grinned and offered, "She's quite a gal, isn't she? I'm lucky to have her."

Squeaking Through

In the Democratic primary, Clinton won a 54.8 per cent of the vote. It was a clear majority, but still considered by many as a "squeaker" finish.

During the primary campaigning, Clinton became aware of an unusual amount of mud-slinging. Rather than flaunting their own political accomplishments and experiences, his challengers had chosen to attack him, both on his public and personal record.

But if the Arkansas governor thought the primary battling was dirty, the fight for against the Republicans was a real mud bath. Businessman Sheffield Nelson knocked off Tommy Robinson to take on Clinton in the election day battle. A former Democrat recently turned Republican, Nelson challenged Clinton on virtually everything he had done since in the governor's office. "He boasts of his contributions to state education," Nelson declared, "and yet our teachers are the lowest paid in the country. He claims significant improvements in the quality of education of our kids. Has anyone looked at their test scores lately? Does Bill Clinton really want to be governor, or is he waiting to board a bus leaving for Washington?"

As the days counted down to Election Day in November of 1990, the Nelson campaign camp released a barrage of political ads. The most damaging was a tape of Clinton speaking before the Arkansas General Assembly. In the speech, he had used–at separate points–the words "raise" and "spend." The Nelson people tied the parts together, repeating the words again and again, as if Clinton was promoting the idea of raising Arkansas taxes to spend, spend, and spend. Frantically, the Democratic team worked to counteract the ads. The phrases from the speech were revealed in true context, and the new ads hailed Clinton as an innovator and builder.

Clinton won out, capturing 59 per cent of the vote. In conceding, Nelson said, "The people said they wanted Bill Clinton for four more years, and I don't think it would have made any difference who was against him. He was just that strong."

Not Wasting Time

For the fifth time, William Jefferson Clinton took the oath of office as Governor of Arkansas. He wasted no time in proposing and endorsing bills that would give scholarships to high school students with at least a B average, increase adult literacy programs, and lift compulsory school attendance from sixteen to seventeen. He wanted drivers under eighteen to have proof of school attendance and he wanted a new apprenticeship work program for non-college-bound high school graduates. He proposed incentives for college medical students who agreed to set up practice in rural areas. He insisted on having social security numbers of both parents on birth certificates, so that any parent neglecting child support payments might be more easily located. A new program for recycling was introduced, and a plan for allowing income tax credit for waste reduction. By most political measurements, it appeared Bill Clinton would need at least four more years to get everything done he planned.

Yet, while Bill Clinton sat working at his governor's desk in Little Rock, a whisper was becoming a shout in other parts of the country. In the air was one word: "Change."

Chapter 8

Making Big Decisions

W hen Ronald Reagan handed over the reins of the presidency to fellow Republican George Bush in January of 1989, the transition was smooth and barely noticeable. Both men were conservatives, of varying degrees, and each believed that the federal government should remain as distant as possible to the lives of the citizens of the United States. "Let us look to the individual to do all that he or she can do," declared Bush, "without the entanglements of government."

With that idea in mind, President Bush took a laidback, unmeddling manner in handling the executive office. His long-time career as a diplomat and government agency director gave him keen insight into international affairs and bureaucracy. He appeared to be well trained to handled the ship of state, and his wife, Barbara, was frequently labeled the most admired woman in the country.

Growing Problems

Yet Americans became increasingly aware of problems going unsolved in the country. Under Reagan and Bush administrations, the national debt had quadrupled to $4 billion The unemployment figures continued to climb, while real estate values tumbled. Law and order became a major concern, as crime statistics rose. Banks and many businesses failed. The sight of a smiling President Bush enjoying the life of luxury at his family compound in Maine distressed many Americans. Perhaps, just perhaps, they thought, it was time for a change.

At the same time, Bill Clinton kept snagging popular media coverage. News of his progressive innovation and streamlining of state programs captured headlines in newspapers and magazines. Noted Washington *Post* columnist David Broder labeled Clinton "a perennially rising star on the national scene," an observation national Democratic chieftains had known for some time. The Arkansas governor became sought after by television and radio commentators and talk show hosts. Even the rival Republicans recognized Clinton's leadership. *Newsweek* magazine, in a June 1991 poll, showed that of the nation's fifty governors, Democrats and Republicans alike, 39 per cent of them thought Bill Clinton was the country's most effective chief executive.

TAKING A POLITICAL PULSE

As chairman of the Democratic Leadership Council, Clinton was able to get a political pulse of party leaders outside the state of Arkansas and other governors. He was the first state chief executive to chair the Council since it began in 1985. Moderate in tone and political philosophy, the group included governors, mayors and legislators. Their goal was to establish good relations between local officials and Congressional Democrats. An article in *Time* magazine noted that "Clinton is the perfect front man for an organization that celebrates the work ethic of the common man while relying almost entirely on the Fortune 500 for operating funds." In other words, Clinton could bridge the gap between management and the working man.

Through his work with the DLC, Clinton sensed the mood of discontent within the country. Whereas he once thought President Bush was unbeatable should he run for the presidency again, Clinton changed his mind. There was a greater feeling among people that Bush was out of tune with Americans, that he was too insulated from how the people felt.

Fighting in Iraq

However, Bush's decisive action against Iraq early in 1991 won the support of a majority of Americans. Iraq's leader, Saddam Hussein, had attacked and annexed the neighboring country of Kuwait. The United Nations, encouraged by Bush and other international leaders, demanded that Iraq withdraw. When Hussein's troops did not do so, fighting broke out.

Despite the backing of the citizens that Bush was receiving against Iraq, Bill Clinton sounded more and more like he planned to challenge the president for his office in 1992. When he visited with 500 elementary children from Little Rock in May of 1991, he said, "I wouldn't mind running, but I haven't made a decision. I'd like to be able to do it someday."

Standing With Pro-Choice

In the summer, Clinton spoke to the National Women's Political Caucus in Washington, D. C. In addressing the abortion issue, the Arkansas governor sounded very much like a candidate for the presidency. He stated that he supported pro-choice views, emphasizing that he thought he shared the feelings of the majority of Americans. "I believe the decision should be the woman's, not the government's," he declared.

As head of the Democratic Leadership Council, Clinton frequently received invitations to speak in other states. There was little doubt that not only was he carrying the message of the DLC, but that he was also testing the waters for a presidential bid.

MAKING THE BIG ANNOUNCEMENT

By October 3, 1991, Bill Clinton had made up his mind. He stood on the steps of the Old State House in Little Rock and looked out at a crowd of 4,500 people. Placards and banners waved and bobbed in the wind. Television cameras clicked away. Music of a high-school band and a college choir set a rousing beat and stirred people's emotions. An historic moment had arrived.

Forty-five-year-old Bill Clinton took his place behind a podium on the main platform. "All of you, in different ways, have brought me here today, to step beyond a life and a job I love, to make a commitment to a large cause: preserving the American Dream, restoring the hopes of the forgotten middle class, reclaiming the future for our children," he announced.

Clinton continued, his oratory pure and polished, his ruddy smooth skin basking in the early afternoon sun. "Middle-class people are spending more hours on the job, spending less time with their children, bringing home a smaller paycheck to pay for more health care and housing and education. Our streets are meaner, our families are more broken, our health care in the costliest in the world and we get less for it."

The people listened, including Hillary and eleven-year-old Chelsea. Occasionally, a spirited fan would yell out "You tell 'em, Bill" and the round of cheers would follow. "We need a new covenant to rebuild America," Clinton declared. "It's just common sense. Government's responsibility is to create more opportunity. The people's responsibility is to make the most of it."

The formal announcement that he was declaring his candidacy for president brought the crowd's loudest cheers. "This is not just a campaign for the presidency," Clinton asserted. "It is a campaign for the future."

Joining the "Six Pack"

Clinton was not the only Democrat who entertained notions about moving into the White House. His party rivals included Jerry Brown, the former governor of California; Tom Harkin, senator from Iowa; Bob Kerry, senator from Nebraska; Paul Tsongas, former senator from Massachusetts; and Douglas Wilder, governor of Virginia. The media nicknamed the six candidates "The Democratic Six-Pack."

New Hampshire, with the first state primary, attracted the candidates like fireflies to a street light. Clinton led a group of devoted friends to the eastern state, and these "Arkansas Travelers" helped set up town meetings and forums.

Fighting the Past

But old skeletons tumbled out of the closet. An article appeared in newspapers around the country bringing back the old Gennifer Flowers affair, and rumors circulated about other encounters with women. Then came stories of how he stayed out of the draft. The tales of smoking pot surfaced too. Badgered by reporters, Clinton tried to answer every controversial question, and the media labeled him "Slick Willie."

That nickname changed on the night of the New Hampshire primary election. In spite of all the sensationalism the media turned up about Clinton, he came in second in the race for delegates, pulling in 25 per cent of the vote. A delighted Clinton labeled himself "The Comeback Kid."

With recharged momentum, Clinton sailed full speed ahead into the campaign. He laid out his plans in a booklet called "A Plan for America's Future," emphasizing the need for economic change and a means to bring back "the American Dream for all."

Wherever he went, Clinton spoke at meetings and forums, challenging the people to "reinvent government." His Arkansas Travelers did much of the leg work, with supporters climbing on the bandwagon. In each state primary, Clinton added to his collection of delegates. One by one his Democratic rivals gave up. Jerry Brown was the last one to abandon the campaign ship. By June of 1992, Clinton had the Democratic nomination locked up.

A Fellow Named Perot

But if Bill Clinton thought he only had to defeat the incumbent President Bush to garner the presidency, he was in for a big surprise. A billionaire Texan named H. Ross Perot entered the political foray as an independent candidate for the top office. Somewhat resembling a leprechaun, Perot won an immediate mass following across the nation with his homespun banter and folksy charm. However, as reporters investigated his past business dealings, questions began being raised as to Perot's character and general stability. He snapped back curt answers when queried, revealing a nasty side to his personality. Soon he lost some of his appeal to the public.

Winning the Nomination

In July, delegates to the Democratic convention in New York City officially nominated William Jefferson Clinton as their candidate for the United States presidency. Clinton, in turn, named Senator Al Gore of Tennessee as his vice-presidential running mate. If elected, the 45-year-old Clinton and the 44-year-old Gore would be the youngest team ever to win the top two seats in government.

Immediately after the Clinton-Gore ticket was chosen, the mischievous Perot stole the spotlight, announcing that he was pulling out as a presidential candidate. His reason? "Now that the Democratic Party has revitalized itself, I have concluded that I cannot win in November." Clinton mobilized his political forces, eager to take on George Bush and Dan Quayle who would be nominated by the Republicans in Au-

"We Want Clinton!" Delegates at the 1992 Democratic National Convention whoop it up in New York City's Madison Square Garden as the presidential candidate savors the exciting moment. (Associated Press.)

gust in Houston, Texas. Before the opposition could gather for their convention, Clinton and Gore took their campaign on a 1,200-mile speaking tour by bus through eight states. The race for the presidential sweepstakes was off and running.

Chapter 9

Into the White House

Candidate Clinton: Are you ready for a change?
    Crowd (yelling): Ye-s-s-
    Clinton: Who has got to go?
Crowd: Bush and Quayle!
Clinton: Who's coming in?
Crowd (shouting hysterically): Clinton and Gore!

It was a familiar script, Clinton igniting enthusiastic supporters in Topeka, Minneapolis, Bettendorf or Cleveland, leading them in chants and cheers. People stood for hours, waiting to welcome the busloads of Clinton/Gore supporters as they barnstormed across America's heartland, rolling over the endless highways. Often, the gatherings were more like high-school pep rallies with jubilant laughter and wild yelling. Large pockets of young adults could be seen in the crowds, with senior citizens and teenagers sprinkled in as well. The spontaneous gatherings posed a major contrast to the well planned and formal conclaves held by the Bush/ Quayle officials.

Clinton seemed well-tuned to the mood of the moment, recognizing that the Americans had lost any joy felt over the country's success against Iraq in the Desert Storm conflict. The nation's debt continued to rise and jobs continued to slip away. With precision and directness, Clinton pointed an accusing finger at the White House. "We need to turn things around," he insisted.

"There will be no change with President Bush in charge."
Suddenly, with just thirty-three days left before the people
headed to the polls, a familiar face raised his head again. Ross
Perot jumped back into the race. "I thought both political
parties would address the problems that face the nation," Perot
claimed. "We gave them the chance. They didn't do it." Perot
picked a retired navy admiral, James Stockdale, as his running mate and pledged some $60,000,000 toward their cam-
paign.

BRING ON THE DEBATES

Once again televised debates promised to be a means of
taking all the candidates to the American people at one time.
Such programs had become a feature of national elections
for many years, and often had a deciding effect on the voters.
Three debates were scheduled, each four days apart.

Clinton knew his biggest weakness was offering too
many details when he spoke. In the opening debate, held October 11 in St. Louis, he managed to keep his answers brief.
He hammered away at the need for change, discussing both
foreign and domestic policy in crisp simple terms. According
to *Time* magazine, Clinton "knew more about more issues
than anyone present." On October 15 in Richmond, Virginia,
the three candidates fielded questions from the studio audience. It had been Clinton's idea to hold such a forum, and he
fired back complete and convincing answers. His plea to those
listening to help him "make America as great as it can be"
was moving and persuasive. The final debate, held in East
Lansing, Michigan, on October 19 gave Clinton a chance to
promise that he was "not going to raise taxes on the middle
class to pay for these taxes." Throughout the campaign, Bush
had been haunted by his pledge uttered four years before over
national television–"Read my lips...no new taxes." Taxes <u>had</u>

President-elect Clinton and Vice President-elect Al Gore, their wives, Hillary Rodham Clinton and Tipper Gore, and their families celebrate final election news in front of the Old Statehouse in Little Rock, Arkansas on November 3, 1992. (Associated Press.)

been raised, however, and many Americans felt doublecrossed.

Polls taken after the debates reflected the public's opinion that Perot had dropped dramatically in public popularity. In a last-minute effort to win voters to his side, the snappy-talking Texan, using graphs and charts, flooded the television screens with half-hour presentations. His status rose, according to surveys shown immediately before the election. It became clear that Perot appeared a stronger candidate without anyone nearby for comparison.

Bush continued to attack Clinton on issues of character. As a World War II veteran, the president kept hitting the draft issue. He warned Americans that Clinton would be a "tax and spend" leader, that he would be reaching constantly into the billfolds of the taxpayers. "Some may call Bill Clinton a New Democrat, but beware–he knows how to spend your money." Other Bush supporters, recognizing that many people found

Hillary Clinton overly aggressive and influential, joked "vote for one, get one free." While Barbara Bush stayed in the background during her husband's political life, Bill Clinton's wife would not likely do the same.

Tallying the Results

But when the voters cast their ballots on November 3, 1992, Bill Clinton racked up 43,728,375 votes to Bush's 38,167,416. Perot trailed with 19,237,247. It was an electoral vote tally of 370 for Clinton, 168 for Bush, and none for Perot. In the popular vote, Clinton captured 43 per cent; Bush, 38 per cent; and Perot, 19 per cent. The newly elected president heard the news in Little Rock, then appeared to make a few remarks. Of the election, Clinton declared it "a victory

President Bill Clinton, with his wife Hillary Rodham Clinton holding the Bible, takes the oath of office from Supreme Court Justice William Rehnquist on January 20, 1993. (Associated Press)

for the people who feel left out and left behind and want to do better, a victory for the people who are ready to compete and win in the global economy but who need a government that offers a hand, not a handout." The man from Hope–and seemingly never without it either–noted, "The American people have voted to make a new beginning."

CLINTON INTRODUCES "NEW BEGINNINGS"

On January 20, 1993, William Jefferson Clinton made his own "new beginning." At forty-six, he was the first president who had been born after World War II. With his wife Hillary beside him, he took the oath of office from Supreme Court Justice William Rehnquist on the West Portico of the U.S. Capitol. Speaking to the crowd, the new chief executive promised "an end to the era of deadlock and draft and a new season of American renewal." Grand inauguration parties followed, with numerous movie and television stars joining the celebration. It was well known that Bill Clinton enjoyed the sparkle and magic of "show biz" atmosphere and glamorous people.

From the moment he was settled into the White House, Clinton was off and running. This time it was not the typical jogging exercises he relied on to keep his weight down and his heart pumping regularly. He was eager to begin, to keep the pledges and promises he had made during his campaign. His old favorite slogan, "You can't lead without listening," echoed through his mind. And he did listen, to countless leaders offering their advice.

Picking a Cabinet

There were some decisions Clinton had to make largely on his own. He had to choose cabinet members, the people who would lead the respective divisions of national government. Certainly he was happy with his vice-president. Noted

On January 22, 1993, the newly-inaugurated President Clinton presents his official cabinet to the press corps as Vice President Gore looks on. (Associated Press.)

for his expertise on defense and the environment, Al Gore had proven to be a major asset on the campaign trail and had become a close friend and confidante. As the second in command of the nation, Gore was the presiding officer in the U.S. Senate. Clinton knew he would be finding other important duties for his able assistant. In selecting his cabinet chiefs, Clinton kept his promise to the voters to make the group look "more like America." Among the eighteen top officials, Clinton selected five women, four African-Americans, and two Latinos. Despite the new president's effort, there were some in the country who grumbled that thirteen of the new cabinet members were lawyers. Clinton grinned and shook his head. "You just can't please everybody," he observed. For better or worse, however, he was determined to try to satisfy as many factions as he could.

Special attention focused on three of the cabinet selections. For his secretary of state, Clinton tapped Warren Christopher. An experienced corporate lawyer, Christopher would advise and oversee foreign affairs. Les Aspin, a longtime and well-liked member of the House of Representatives, was selected to head the Defense Department. The position of Attorney General proved to be the most difficult to fill. Clinton's first nominee, an insurance executive named Zoe Baird, turned out to have employed an illegal alien couple in her home, thereby violating a 1986 immigration law. Hardly appropriate for the nation's "top cop," Baird withdrew from consideration, being replaced by another woman nominee, U. S. District Court Judge Kimba Wood. Investigations revealed that she, too, had employed an illegal alien as a baby-sitter, although at the time it was not breaking a law. Backing away from Wood's nomination, Clinton finally selected Florida's chief prosecutor in Miami, Janet Reno. She proved a popular choice, sailing through a unanimous Senate confirmation March 11 and taking the oath of office the following day.

Controversy over Clinton's nomination of University of Pennsylvania law professor Lani Guinier as assistant attorney general in charge of civil rights enforcement erupted quickly. Conservatives branded her a "quota queen" based on her published legal writings which constantly advocated minority numbers and influence. After admitting he had not read her articles, Clinton dropped her nomination, promising to keep "a closer eye" on such matters.

Finding a Judge

Clinton's nomination of Ruth Bader Ginsberg to the U. S. Supreme Court to replace the retiring Associate Justice Byron White seemed to show he meant what he said. For the former judge of the court of appeals in the District of Columbia Ginsberg won easy Senate approval by a vote of 96-3 in

August of 1993 and became the Supreme Court's 117th justice.

Long concerned with the behavior of top officials within the executive branch, Clinton issued an order imposing higher standards of conduct. He also overturned five major restrictions on abortions which had been set into place by the previous Republican administrations. Pro- choice leaders applauded the new president, while pro-lifers condemned his action. On February 5, 1993, Clinton signed family leave legislation, allowing government workers and employees of companies having fifty or more workers, up to twelve weeks of unpaid leave

On June 15, 1993, President Clinton applauds as Judge Ruth Bader Ginsburg prepares to speak in the White House Rose Garden. Nominated to fill the post of retiring Justice Byron White, Ginsburg sailed through confirmation hearings and took her place on the United States Supreme Court later in the summer. (Associated Press.)

The Original Cabinet of President Bill Clinton

Secretary of State - Warren Christopher
Secretary of Treasury - Lloyd Bentsen
Secretary of Defense - Les Aspin
Attorney General - Janet Reno
Secretary of the Interior - Bruce Babbitt
Secretary of Agriculture - Mike Espy
Secretary of Commerce - Ronald H. Brown
Secretary of Labor - Robert B. Reich
Secretary of Health and Human Services - Donna E. Shalala
Secretary of Housing and Urban Development - Henry Cisneros
Secretary of Transportation - Federico Pena
Secretary of Energy - Hazel R. O'Leary
Secretary of Education - Richard W. Riley
Secretary of Veterans Affairs - Jesse Brown

In addition to the fourteen cabinet positions listed above, President Clinton named four additional individuals as cabinet level appointments.
Director of the Environmental Protection Agency - Carol M. Browner
Director of Office Management and Budget - Leon E. Panetta
Special Trade Representative - Mickey Kantor
United Nations Ambassador - Madeleine K. Albright

to care for personal Health-care benefits would be covered by the employers, and workers returning to their jobs were guaranteed their positions back. President Bush had twice vetoed similar legislation.

Offering a Plan

While campaigning, Clinton promised, if elected, to make his first 100 days in office "The most productive period in modern history." Proposed bills would be heading to Congress "quickly and efficiently." Speaking before Congress on February 16, less than a month after his inauguration, the new president laid out "a comprehensive plan" to set the national course. He included plans to create jobs for the unemployed, plans to streamline the budget and cut the deficit, plans for educational reform, and plans to tighten defense spending.

One of Clinton's initial proposals that met fierce opposition was a proposed change in the military ban on homosexuals. Senator Sam Nunn, Chairman of the Armed Services Committee, and the Joint Chiefs of Staff voiced strong opposition to Clinton's suggested changes. An "honorable compromise" was quickly reached that military recruits would not be asked their sexual orientation upon induction. The "don't ask, don't tell, don't pursue" philosophy allowed gays to serve in the military as long as they followed the rules and fulfilled their duties. The joint chiefs announced their support of the compromise, but gay rights leaders felt that the president had backed down on his campaign pledge to lift all restrictions.

Chapter 10
Riding the Presidential Rollercoaster

C linton found a special job for his wife Hillary. He named her to head a task force focused on health care and health insurance. Almost 37 million Americans were without health insurance, a statistic that Clinton labeled "shocking and impossible to accept." Hillary Rodham Clinton set up an office in the West Wing of the White House from which to operate. Her goal was to put together a program that offered health-care coverage to everyone, yet kept the costs done. It was noted that Americans spend approximately $800 million yearly on health care.

Despite his promises to speed up the passage of bills through Congress, Clinton soon discovered things just did not move that fast. Nor could he fulfill all of the pledges made during the campaign. His aides discovered higher deficit projections than they expected, and the promise of reducing the deficit by 50 per cent in four years was not possible. The plan to cut taxes for the middle class also proved unrealistic. Clinton's hopes of submitting a plan to Congress for comprehensive health care quickly were delayed due to the critical illness of Hillary Clinton's father.

Tough Lessons in Leading

The "honeymoon" period between the new president and Congress slipped away quickly. Americans were little impressed with Clinton's decision to hold up a flight of Air Force One while he received a $200 haircut from a Beverly Hills hairdresser at Los Angeles International Airport. The White House suffered further embarrassment when it became known that people from Arkansas had been imported to run the internal travel office and seven experienced staff members were dismissed. When a top official from the State Department declared publicly that the United States would no longer assume a leadership role in world affairs, more people shook their heads in disbelief. In April, after only four months in office, Clinton's popularity plummeted to 40 per cent, a startlingly low approval rating. David Gergen, a public relations specialist and former assistant to President Ronald Reagan, was pulled aboard the Clinton staff to help the slipping administration image.

"I wish the media would allow us to focus on the mountains, not the molehills," an annoyed Clinton said. "We have much to do, and important matters of the nation need to receive all our time and talents."

MONEY MATTERS

Backing up his remarks, Clinton concentrated on a major economic stimulus package amounting to over $16 billion Included in the program were means of creating new jobs, funding public work projects, increasing social welfare services, and aiding education. Republicans attacked the Clinton bill, claiming it would do little to help the economy but it would only increase the deficit. A total of sixty Senate votes were needed to pass the package, and the Republicans kept the bill from passing.

Their muscles flexed, Republicans then focused on Clinton's proposals to reduce the deficit. The new president presented legislation that included tax hikes and an tax, wearing a $493 billion price tag. Like a rag doll the deficit-reduction package was tossed around, compromised, discussed, negotiated, and patched up. Clinton learned much about Washington politics, discovering that he could not automatically count on fellow Democrats to support his legislation. With $255 billion in spending cuts and $240 billion in tax increases, the package slithered through the House of Representatives with a 218-216 vote. It passed in the Senate 51-50, thanks to the tie-breaking vote of Vice-President Gore.

Supporting an Old Enemy

On the international front, Clinton offered both moral and financial support to Russian President Boris Yeltsin. At a summit meeting held in Vancouver, Canada, early in April, Clinton carried a $1,600,000,000 foreign aid package to the leader, and helped pave the way for an additional $43,000,000,000 from seven other industrial nations. Not only was the American aid a major shot in the arm to Russian

President Clinton and Russian President Boris Yeltsin shake hands in September of 1994 after signing agreements pledging closer economic and security cooperation. The meetings between the two leaders were held at the White House. (Associated Press.)

economy, but Clinton's personal support help boost Yeltsin's prestige among his own people.

BOSNIA REMAINS AN OPEN WOUND

Critical of President Bush's handling of the civil war in Bosnia, Clinton discovered the situation was more complex than he had initially realized. Serbian forces continued an offensive military attack, specializing in snipeshooting and hit-and-run assaults, hoping to achieve some degree of force and authority. Clinton threw the support of the United States behind United Nations and North Atlantic Treaty Organization (NATO) efforts to achieve a cease fire and some sort of settlement between Serbs and Croats. One popular U.N. plan would have divided Bosnia and Herzegovina into regions based on ethnic makeup. A self-proclaimed Bosnian Serb parliament rejected that effort. Economic sanctions against Yugoslavia froze the country's assets abroad and banned shipment in and out of the country, by land or water. The fighting within Yugoslavia continued. Some Americans questioned the need to be involved, yet photos of starving prisoners in war camps brought memories of similar sights from World War II and continued to bring an outburst of humanitarian concern. Clinton stuck to a position of backing the United Nations and NATO forces in the struggle. "We cannot turn our backs on those crying out for our help," the president insisted.

A LONG, HOT SUMMER

Early in July, Clinton dismissed William Sessions, Director of the Federal Bureau of Investigation. Both Sessions and his wife had been accused of tax abuses, and Attorney Janet Reno pressured the FBI chief to resign. He refused, and Clinton fired him. U. S. District Court Judge Louis J. Freeh was tapped by Clinton to replace Sessions and won quick and unanimous conformation in the Senate.

Later in July of 1993, the Clinton family suffered a personal loss when longtime personal friend and deputy White House counsel Vincent Foster was found shot to death in a park in northern Virginia. Foster and the counsel's office had been criticized for the handling of presidential nominations and the controversy over the White House travel agency. Although Foster's death was deemed a suicide, suspicions arose to his knowledge and actions involving Whitewater, an Arkansas real estate venture in which both Bill and Hillary Clinton were involved.

WHITEWATER PROVES TO BE MUDDY WATERS

Throughout the Clinton presidency, the Whitewater affair cast a grim shadow of suspicion. An intense investigation led by special counsel Robert Fiske and released in April 1994 revealed no evidence of criminal wrongdoing by anyone in the White House, including President and Mrs. Clinton. But such revelations did little to dispel the public suspicions of some degree of wrongdoing.

Stories about Whitewater had surfaced during Clinton's campaign for the presidency. Accusers suggested that while Clinton was governor of Arkansas, he had improperly used his office in real estate transactions known as "Whitewater." The Clintons had invested in an ill- fated northern Arkansas vacation-home development. "I never would have participated in the investment in the first place if I'd known what was going to happen later," declared Hillary Rodham Clinton.

But invest the Clintons did, some sixteen years earlier, and their business dealings came back to haunt them. A New York *Times* reporter, Jeff Gerth, broke the story in March of 1992, relating how the Clintons had become equal partners with another Arkansas couple, James and Susan McDougal, in the Whitewater Development Corporation. McDougal later owned an Arkansas Savings and Loan named Madison Guaranty, which Hillary Clinton represented in dealings with the state of Arkansas. Critics argued she should not have dealt with state regulators appointed by her husband, the governor.

At first, it seemed those doing the accusing were disgruntled Republican office-seekers in Arkansas. Yet the situation clearly became much more than that. Charges flew of abuse of political power, fraud, illegal use of funds–and despite Clinton's denials of wrongdoing, the problem grew bigger. A grand jury convened to hear a long parade of witnesses, and several government employees resigned after being accused of cover-up efforts. "The facts of the matter will probably never be known," observed one political expert, "yet there will always be a cloud over the Clintons and their presidency."

An Eye to the Environment

Responding to his vice-president's concern for the environment, Clinton convened a forest summit to resolve a complex dispute over protection of the spotted owl in the Northwestern state. The president also received praise for creating a White House Office of Environmental Policy.

Another type of environmental crisis captured Clinton's attention during the summer of 1993. The president flew to the Midwest to review the damages caused by devastating floods. Past seasonal rains had left the ground saturated, and the excess waters swelled the Mississippi and other rivers to overflowing. Dikes and levees crumbled, and tap water was declared unsafe to drink. All of Iowa and major portions of eight other states were declared "disaster areas" as the angry floods claimed fifty lives and left tens of thousands homeless.

Two Leaders Meet

On August 12, Clinton flew to Denver where he officially welcomed Pope John Paul II to the United States. The Roman Catholic leader took part in a Catholic Youth Convo-

Playing chauffeur to daughter Chelsea, President Clinton smoothly navigates his vintage Mustang convertible to his 47th birthday party held in Little Rock. The sunglasses and letter sweater were part of the party festivities. (Associated Press.)

cation. A second trip to the United States, scheduled for the fall of 1994, had to be cancelled when the Pope, 74, was not well enough to make the journey.

In September of 1993, Clinton and Gore proved a close partnership, in announcing proposed plans to "Reinvent Government." They had made the pledge often during their campaigning, and they offered a blueprint to streamline the federal government. This broad program included 800 recommendations with a potential savings of $108,000,000,000 over a five-year period. Among the provisions were to cut federal jobs by 252,000 and to close many regional offices of federal departments.

On September 13, 1993, President Clinton hosted an historic ceremony when he presided at a peace agreement signing at the White House. Israeli leader Yitzak Rabin and Palestine Liberation Organization Yasir Arafat came together to agree on a framework of unity designed to promote peaceful cooperation between their people. Although the United States had played no major pivotal role in bringing the longtime enemies together, Clinton pledged that his country would play an active role in working out a final, workable peace plan as well as doing everything possible in the Mideast to make the pact politically viable.

A BIG VICTORY

Later that same month, Clinton forcefully tackled another major economic challenge. Originally assembled during the Bush administration, the North Atlantic Free Trade Agreement (NAFTA) erased all tariffs among the United States, Canada and Mexico. Many Democrats, especially those representing large blocks of union members, opposed the agreement, fearing the loss of jobs to Mexicans. Ross Perot jumped into the squabbling, too, publishing and circulating a book against NAFTA. Nonetheless, Clinton stood firm, exerting all the political muscle he could muster. Some members of Congress hailed the agreement, claiming the United States had everything to gain and nothing to lose by free trade. Former Presidents Gerald Ford, Jimmy Carter, and George Bush visited the White House at Clinton's request and endorsed NAFTA. Critics still blasted away at the trade agreement, stating that it would greatly harm the nation's work force. When the shouting ended and the votes were all counted in Congress, Clinton emerged the victor, showing those who doubted that he still knew how to play political hardball against major adversaries.

Sharing a Health Care Plan

It was not until September 22, 1993, that Clinton was

prepared to publicly unveil the health care program he had advocated during his presidential campaign. Since her appointment to lead health care reform in January, Hillary Rodham Clinton and her team had listened to professionals in the area before drawing up their final proposals. The reform program was projected to cost the federal program $350,000,000,000 over seven years. Funding would come from savings in Medicare and Medicaid as well as other health programs. An additional tax would be placed on tobacco. All American citizens and legal aliens would be covered, primarily through employers picking up 80 per cent of the health insurance costs of full-time employees. Congressional members were stunned at the depth and breadth of the plan. Clearly, it would take many months of discussion and debate before any final action could be taken. Even if passed immediately, an initial target date of 1997 for implementation was considered premature by most governmental leaders. Hillary Clinton and her aides knew they had much more to do in creating a practical health care reform package. They promised to bring back a more concrete and comprehensive proposal in 1994.

The National Service Bill backed by Clinton won Senate approval 57-40 in September, allowing participants to receive grants for up to two years by performing community service supervised by nonprofit national and state agencies, colleges and other groups. Twenty thousand students would be funded the first year, for up to $4,725 annually.

President Clinton, accompanied by former presidents Gerald Ford, Jimmy Carter and George Bush, gather in the White House in September of 1993 for a side-deal signing of the three-nation North American Free Trade Agreement. The full NAFTA bill passed in the fall of 1994. (Associated Press.)

Chapter 11

Keeping the Peace

I n 1981, President's Reagan's press secretary, James Brady, was crippled during an assassination attempt against the chief executive. Almost immediately, legislation appeared which attempted to make it more difficult to purchase handguns, one of which was used in the attack.

One of the pieces of legislation that received the greatest popular support was the Brady Bill, which imposed a five day waiting period on the purchase of any handgun. In 1987, James Brady and his wife, Sarah, became lobbyists for the bill, winning widespread popular citizen support.

President Clinton endorsed the Brady Bill and rallied support around it. Opponents, including Republican Senate leader Bob Dole and the powerful National Rifle Association, voiced concerns that the Brady Bill was only symbolic and would not keep handguns out of the hands of criminals or anyone else who would misuse them. But in November of 1993, the Republicans dropped their opposition and the legislation passed, taking effect in February of 1994.

Pushing Another Anti-Crime Bill

After the passage of the Brady Bill, sensing the mood of the nation, Clinton spent the early part of 1994 focusing on ways and means of increasing law and order through effective legislation. By summer, new legislation offered increased funds, at least on a temporary basis, for additional police officers as well as an extended waiting period for gun purchases and more prisons. "We must make our streets safe," Clinton asserted. "Our citizens should not have to live in fear of losing their lives or their property." Lawmakers squabbled back and forth, offering revisions and modifications to Clinton's initial offerings. In late August, the House voted 235-195 to back the proposals, while the Senate followed suit, 61-39, three weeks later.

Always looking for ways to improve education, Clinton backed a school reform bill entitled Goals 2000. "The central value of this legislation is that it allows us to work for bettering education both nationally and locally," declared Clinton. Financially, the bill authorized $647,000,000 for school reforms nationwide, including $400,000,000 in grants to states and local school agencies. The funds were designed to help evaluate and improve educational programs.

The House of Representatives debated Goals 2000 for five days, before voting 306-121 to send it to the Senate. Despite a filibuster led by Senator Jesse Helms, the Senate passed the legislation 63-22.

Shifting Positions

As a candidate for the presidency, Clinton had threatened to hit China with trade sanctions if he was elected, unless the Chinese government improved its poor human rights policies. Upon careful examination, Clinton "delinked" China's trade status from human rights and asked Congress to renew the country's most favored nation trading status. That status allows exports into the United States at the lowest tariff available.

"Human rights are relevant," declared Clinton, in announcing his shift in position, "but they are outweighed by an inescapable reality–the tone of our relations must shift from confrontational to cooperation as our two nations move toward a new century that could see China become an economic superpower. China's economy is the world's third largest, and trade between the United States and China is worth tens of billions of dollars a year to both nations."

Stopping the Flow

In August of 1994, President Clinton turned back nearly thirty years of Cuban policy. The constant flow of refugees willing to risk the treacherous 90-mile crossing from their homeland to Florida had increased sharply in the last few years. American officials had tried warnings and threats, but still the Cubans came.

President Clinton shares speaking duties with Nelson Mandela, president of South Africa's African National Congress. Held as a political prisoner for 27 years, Mandela led the fight for free elections in his homeland during April of 1994, an event Clinton hailed as "a major step for democracy." (Associated Press.)

A "Brief" History of Clinton

Did she really ask that question? Surely not. And yet, a glance at the silver-maned fellow who stood grinning at the podium confirmed that she had indeed asked the question.

The scene was an MTV youth forum in April of 1994. The questioner was 17 year-old Laetitia Thompson, a high school student. The question? "The world is dying to know, Mr. President," queried Miss Thompson, "if you wear briefs or boxers?"

President Clinton did not skirt the question. He informed the audience present as well as the millions more watching the junior press conference that he wears briefs. Such a revelation probably came as little surprise to the folks of his home state. In Arkansas, briefs outsell boxer shorts 5 to 1, 400 million pairs a year to 80 million, with bikini drawers snuggling in a distant third.

But perhaps more important that it was asked was the fact that it was asked at all. Would the question have been asked Clinton's predecessor, President George Bush? Probably not. Then why would a high school student ask President Clinton?

"I wouldn't say 'the world is dying to know,' " noted another 17 year-old high school student Jason Moskowitz who watched the televised interview. "But the fact that the question was asked — and even more importantly, that it was answered — showed that my generation is straightforward and that President Clinton does not put the Presidency on some out-of-reach pedestal. I think it also shows he has a sense of humor."

William Kristol, former chief of staff to Vice-President Dan Quayle, disagreed with Clinton's willingness to reply. "There is a dignity to the office that must be maintained," Kristol insisted. "This, after all, is the elected head of our nation, a man who represents leadership in both domestic and foreign policy. Should

he be talking about his underwear publicly? I think not."
 Another 17-year-old high school student sided with
Moskowitz. "It was not as if the president was addressing Congress or the United Nations, " observed Josh
Ford after the interview. "He was talking in an MTV
surrounding, hanging out with a bunch of young people.
By being there, or by going on the Arsenio Hall Show
and playing his saxophone, the president shows he
wants to reach all kinds of people. As young people, we
appreciate that. After all, he is our president too."
 The Los Angeles *Times*, often at odds with Clinton
over policies and issues, offered the chief executive
support in this area. The editors conceded that Clinton's
accessibility is "part of his charm."
 "Clinton's admission that he wears briefs is hardly
headline news," concluded Moskowitz. "And I don't
think we'll start a 'boxer rebellion' over it."

Finally, Clinton stepped in. He went on television and
publicly revoked the special status Cuban refugees have
enjoyed for three decades, a status guaranteeing them
asylum if they reached the United States. Instead, Cuban
refugees faced indefinite detention while immigration officials reviewed their cases. Within weeks, the numbers of refugees dramatically declined.

FORMER PRESIDENT RETURNS AS PEACEMAKER

In both the summer and fall of 1994, President Clinton
called on one of the former presidents to represent the
country's interests in major confrontations. Former chief executive Jimmy Carter had been spending much of his time
helping construct housing for the poor, but he quickly slipped
out of his carpenter's workclothes and into his formal diplomatic attire at Clinton's request.

First, it was North Korea in June. Known as the largest

exporter of Scud missiles, the small but mighty Asian power began making ugly threats, suggesting it would soon pursue and expand a program to manufacture nuclear weapons. Kim Il Sung, dictator of North Korea for forty-six years, seemed dogged and determined in his plans. Most concerned was Kim Young Sam, president of the Republic of Korea, North Korea's neighbor to the south. Wasting no time, President Clinton enlisted the services of former President Carter, who headed for North Korea's capital, Pyongyang. Carter pulled Sung and Young together, and helped negotiate a peaceful resolution. That negotiation included closer diplomatic and financial ties between North Korea and the United States, including the latter's plans to dismantle the existing atomic reactor at Pyongyang for a price tag of over $1,000,000,000. "That's a lot of money," observed one American diplomat, "but North Korea could cause a lot of trouble producing nuclear bombs."

TROUBLE IN HAITI

Having barely unpacked his bags from the North Korea mission, Carter was again tapped by President Clinton for peacemaking duties–this time in the Caribbean island of Haiti.

Following the election of Jean-Bertrand Aristide to the presidency of Haiti, a military junta led by army commander Lieutenant General Raoul Cedras drove the democratically elected leader from power. Reports of the brutality of the Haitian police filtered out of the country. Throughout the summer, Clinton attempted to apply pressure on the self-imposed leadership, including the freezing of Haitian financial assets in the United States. "We should keep on the table the option of forcibly removing the dictators who have usurped power in Haiti," Clinton declared. Although Cedras and his colleagues refused to give in, Clinton's actions did cause major dissension among the Haitian leadership. Rumors persisted of a possible break within the junta.

By late summer, Clinton's patience had reached an end. His threats of a United States invasion went ignored. Government officials bickered about reported offers of millions of dollars for the military junta to step down and leave the country. Cedras defiantly declared that he would never leave Haiti.

In September, Clinton had taken all he could. "Your time is up," he told Cedras and his cohorts. "Leave now, or we will force you from power." American soldiers were dispatched to the Caribbean and invaded the island. Lieutenant General Hugh Henry Shelton, commander of the U. S. occupation force, declared "Our forces are here to maintain order and stability, not to shed blood. However, there will be no more police violence."

Enter Former President Carter, accompanied by retired General Colin Powell, former joint chiefs chairman and Senator Sam Nunn, chairman of the Armed Services Committee. Arriving at the island's capital, Port-au- Prince, the three Americans began nonstop meetings with the Haitian officials. Carefully and firmly they negotiated, setting up terms for the junta to give up power and return the government into the hands of President Aristide. Cedras and the others agreed to leave the country and relinquish their power. Within weeks, the agreement was put into effect, Aristide was back in power, and both Clinton and Carter won praise for their efforts in international diplomacy.

Chapter 12

Into the Future

S ince assuming office in January of 1993, President Clinton pushed, prodded, and pulled to have
political leaders and the American people get behind
a program of national health care. With his wife, Hillary, as
its chief proponent, every effort was made to bring accept-
able legislation before Congress. Blockades popped up constantly, many of them championed by Senator Bob Dole of
Kansas, the Republican leader who said, "The Clinton health
care plan, whether one calls it Bill's or Hillary's, is a massive
overdose of government control."

President Clinton fired back at his critics. "We need to
give every hardworking American the same health-care security they have already given us," declared Clinton, in his
State of Union Address to the country's lawmakers on January 25, 1994. The chief executive even threatened Congress,
promising that if the legislation they sent to him for his sig-
nature "does not guarantee every American private health insurance that can never be taken away, you will force me to
take this pen, veto that legislation and we'll come right back
here and start over."

Months of discussion and argument followed, with supporters and attackers debating the merits and drawbacks of
proposed health care. Much of the health care program was
put together by business consultant Ira Magaziner, working

side-by-side with Hillary Clinton. Her staff grew to 500 workers who collected data and wrote proposals and possible legislation. Once the overall program was ready to take before the public, health care proponents boarded a bus dubbed "The Health Security Express" and headed across the country picking up other supporters, then headed back to Washington where they could take their message to lawmakers. Compromises were suggested, some accepted and others rejected. Senate Majority Leader George Mitchell added a number of amendments to the original legislation, many of which won acceptance The final document reaching Congress contained 1342 pages and weighed four pounds. Both lawmakers and their constituents back home found the suggested reforms too complex and impossible to deal with, yet the door was left open for action in the future. "It's certainly not a dead issue," observed Senator Harris Woffold of Pennsylvania, "but it's something we need to sleep on a bit."

America's financial and economic picture brightened in the fall with announcement of unemployment figures sinking to 6.7. Inflation figures also continued to slip. Government officials announced a modest 2.6 per cent increase for Social Security recipients in 1994, the second smallest annual rise since benefit payments were linked to inflation in 1975. However, when the Federal Reserve Board announced a raise in interest rates of three quarters of a per cent in November, Clinton and others wore few smiles.

Clinton Raps Saddam Hussain's Knuckles

An old adversary raised his head again in October of 1994. Iraq's leader, Saddam Hussain, surprisingly quiet since being squelched in the 1991 Desert Storm encounter with the United States, resurfaced by sending 20,000 fresh troops into neighboring Kuwait. Ordering Hussain to withdraw his soldiers immediately, Clinton also sought a United Nations Security Council resolution demanding Iraq pull out of Kuwait. Clinton got his wish, and the president also jumped to a 61% public approval rating of his handling of the Iraq situation.

REPUBLICANS POST MIDTERM VICTORIES

In the off-year elections held in November of 1994, Republicans won control of the United States House of Representatives by picking up 52 seats and the United States Senate by winning eight additional spots. Republicans also gained eleven Governors' mansions. The balloting was seen as a general rejection of President Clinton and his policies as well as a distinct move away from the Democrats. "This was more than an election," said Toby Roth, a new Republican Representative from Wisconsin. "It was a revolution."

Whatever the case, Clinton showed little concern over the low poll ratings of his job performance–hovering around 40 per cent–through much of 1994. He felt proud of his efforts to reduce crime through increased funds for police and prisons, increased gun control, family leave, and NAFTA, eliminating 70,000 federal jobs and reducing the budget deficit. "People sometimes tend to overlook accomplishments," Clinton says. "Every president in a transition period in our history who's fought for real change has had to face the risk of unpopularity. My frustration is whether I have succeeded or failed in communicating to the American people."

A Peek into the Future

What does the future hold? Clinton is optimistic. As president, he declares, "I've got to keep modernizing the economy. We've also got to deal with two great legislative items, health care reform and welfare reform. We have still got to change the way the government works. People often don't have confidence in it."

How the major Republican comeback in the midterm

President Clinton briefs Congressional leaders on Operation Uphold Democracy in Haiti in September of 1994. From left are Defense Secretary William Perry, Joint Chiefs Chairman General John Shalikashvili, Clinton, Secretary of State Warren Christopher, House Majority Whip David Bonior and House Speaker Thomas Foley. (Associated Press.)

elections of 1994 will affect the Clinton presidency remains to be seen. Senate Republican leader Bob Dole, often a critic and adversary, joined the president in supporting the General Agreements of Tariffs and Treaties (GATT) legislation, reflecting some degree of bipartisan cooperation. "I am willing to work with anyone," Clinton asserts, "as long as they are working for the people. That, after all, is what a democracy is all about."

Bibliography

Allen, Charles F. and Jonathan Portis. *The Comeback Kid.* New York: Birch Lane Press. 1992. This adult biography traces the life of Bill Clinton, focusing in depth upon the political dimensions. Clearly, the man is one who does not give up, but instead seeks fresh energy and plans to lift himself onto new roads. Both Clinton's strengths and weaknesses are carefully examined objectively. Photos of a young Clinton growing up are especially fascinating.

Farmighetti, Robert. *World Almanac and Book of Facts 1994*, Mahwah, New Jersey: Funk and Wagnalls. 1993. Two sections of this almanac are especially useful–one covering a general overview of national, international and general events, and another which offers a capsule report of first year of the Clinton Presidency.

Gallen, David (with Philip Martin). *Bill Clinton As They Knew Him* New York: Gallen Publishing Group. 1994. Bill Clinton is remembered in personal anecdotes supplied by people who have known him all through his life. He emerges as an ambitious and hardworking man, with a constant desire to satisfy everyone he can.

Hohenberg, John. *The Bill Clinton Story : Winning the Presidency*, Syracuse, New York: Syracuse University Press. 1994. Hohenberg's volume steps beyond the confines of a typical biography by carefully analyzing the ways and means of winning the top office in the United States, Clinton-style. It's almost a "how to" book for politicians of the future who share Bill Clinton's hopes and dreams.

Kent, Zachary. *William Jefferson Clinton.* Chicago: Children's Press. 1993. The latest in the Encyclopedia of Presidents Series, this volume includes the life of Bill Clinton to the point of his inauguration in January of 1993. Young readers who enjoy many photographs will appreciate this offering which is filled with facts and moves swiftly through a well-written text.

Levin, Robert E. *Bill Clinton : The Inside Story,* New York: S.P.I. Books. 1992. Bill Clinton's rise from a modest beginning in Hope, Arkansas and ending in the White House comes to life thanks to the revealing commentary of so many people who shared the exciting road with him. Classmates, neighbors, political associates, friends - the remembrances of those who knew him offers understanding and insight into a complex and competitive human product of post-World War II days.

Radcliffe, Donnie. *Hillary Rodham Clinton.* New York: Warner Books, 1993. Few presidential wives have been covered by the media so extensively as Bill Clinton's First Lady. This book helps explain why. Hillary Rodham Clinton is an intense, focused woman whom people in this biography recall with a variety of feelings, few of them neutral or subtle.

Woodward, Bob. *The Agenda: Inside the Clinton White House.* New York: Simon & Schuster. 1994. Efficiency and effectiveness are clearly not Bill Clinton's strong points as far as running an organized administrative team, if one accepts this look at the Clinton staff. It offers a critical and penetrating look at why the administration has problems communicating their message not only to the public but even to each other.

Index

PRESIDENTS OF THE
UNITED STATES

GEORGE WASHINGTON	L. Falkof	0-944483-19-4
JOHN ADAMS	R. Stefoff	0-944483-10-0
THOMAS JEFFERSON	R. Stefoff	0-944483-07-0
JAMES MADISON	B. Polikoff	0-944483-22-4
JAMES MONROE	R. Stefoff	0-944483-11-9
JOHN QUINCY ADAMS	M. Greenblatt	0-944483-21-6
ANDREW JACKSON	R. Stefoff	0-944483-08-9
MARTIN VAN BUREN	R. Ellis	0-944483-12-7
WILLIAM HENRY HARRISON	R. Stefoff	0-944483-54-2
JOHN TYLER	L. Falkof	0-944483-60-7
JAMES K. POLK	M. Greenblatt	0-944483-04-6
ZACHARY TAYLOR	D. Collins	0-944483-17-8
MILLARD FILLMORE	K. Law	0-944483-61-5
FRANKLIN PIERCE	F. Brown	0-944483-25-9
JAMES BUCHANAN	D. Collins	0-944483-62-3
ABRAHAM LINCOLN	R. Stefoff	0-944483-14-3
ANDREW JOHNSON	R. Stevens	0-944483-16-X
ULYSSES S. GRANT	L. Falkof	0-944483-02-X
RUTHERFORD B. HAYES	N. Robbins	0-944483-23-2
JAMES A. GARFIELD	F. Brown	0-944483-63-1
CHESTER A. ARTHUR	R. Stevens	0-944483-05-4
GROVER CLEVELAND	D. Collins	0-944483-01-1
BENJAMIN HARRISON	R. Stevens	0-944483-15-1
WILLIAM McKINLEY	D. Collins	0-944483-55-0
THEODORE ROOSEVELT	R. Stefoff	0-944483-09-7
WILLIAM H. TAFT	L. Falkof	0-944483-56-9
WOODROW WILSON	D. Collins	0-944483-18-6
WARREN G. HARDING	A. Canadeo	0-944483-64-X
CALVIN COOLIDGE	R. Stevens	0-944483-57-7

HERBERT C. HOOVER	B. Polikoff	0-944483-58-5
FRANKLIN D. ROOSEVELT	M. Greenblatt	0-944483-06-2
HARRY S. TRUMAN	D. Collins	0-944483-00-3
DWIGHT D. EISENHOWER	R. Ellis	0-944483-13-5
JOHN F. KENNEDY	L. Falkof	0-944483-03-8
LYNDON B. JOHNSON	L. Falkof	0-944483-20-8
RICHARD M. NIXON	R. Stefoff	0-944483-59-3
GERALD R. FORD	D. Collins	0-944483-65-8
JAMES E. CARTER	D. Richman	0-944483-24-0
RONALD W. REAGAN	N. Robbins	0-944483-66-6
GEORGE H.W. BUSH	R. Stefoff	1-56074-033-7
WILLIAM J. CLINTON	D. Collins	1-56074-056-6

GARRETT EDUCATIONAL CORPORATION
130 EAST 13TH STREET
ADA, OK 74820